Linda

Hi Table B...

Thanks for all of the

wonderful conversation.

You are truly a

remarkable lady"!

Stay in touch' !

Love,

Jann Gaymer

# Becoming

# Unmarried

## Navigating Divorce with Grace (for the most part) and Humor

by Tami Jayne

# Becoming Unmarried

The methods described within this book are the author's personal thoughts. They are not intended to be a definitive set of instructions. You may discover there are other methods and materials to accomplish the same end result. To protect the privacy of certain individuals the names and some identifying details have been changed.

Published 2017
Printed in the United States of America

ISBN 978-1-939294-48-7

Published by splatteredinkpress.com

### *To Daddy*

Watching me go through this was hard on you, as was losing someone you considered to be your son.

But you helped me through this as much, if not more, than anyone else.

I now know there truly is no man out there who takes care of me the way only my father can.

You are my hero, and I cannot thank you enough for being there for your little girl.

I love you.
Now go play in the garden.

# Acknowledgments

*Mom*

Like Daddy, I'm not sure I can ever thank you enough for all you have done. Mom is always right, and I should have listened to you more. I love you, too.

*Amy*

Here I thought as the Big Sister it was my job to look out for you. Glad you never listened to me when we were kids and I told you to get lost, as I surely would have been lost without you going through this whole ordeal.

Even though you are still a brat, you're my brat, so deal with it. ☺

*The Besties*

Yep, you ladies are the best. I can't merely call you 'my girlfriends,' as you are so much more than that.

Shannon, Lisa, Sandi, Gena, Jennifer & Elizabeth.

You may come from different places and situations, but I'm eternally grateful I had you ladies to come together when I needed you most.

Stay strong, smart and beautiful.

The next round is on me!

*Tricia*

The Editor – and so much more!

Thanks for pushing me to tell my story and for acting as a surrogate therapist when I needed to get my emotions out there and down on paper.

Also, thank you for being patient during the editing process and finally telling the Gremlins to beat it so I could get this book done!

*Team Tami*

My co-workers, mentors, professionals, family and friends. You are too numerous to list, but know you each played a major part in my growth and have helped me tell my story.

Thank you for being my safety net.

Since this section is called Acknowledgements, I guess I need to give some credit to the reason behind this book.

S.

I think The Clash said it best,

*You didn't stand by me*
*No, not at all*
*You didn't stand by me*
*No way*

As it turns out, I didn't need you to stand by me.
In fact, you were right.
In leaving me, you did indeed do me a favor.
So... *thank you*

# Table of Contents

# Chapter One

## Dear Reader

"Do you solemnly swear to tell the truth,
the whole truth and nothing but the truth;
so help you God?"

This was the question the judge asked my husband as he prepared to take the stand at one of our court dates in the fall of 2013. Since I was the defendant, I never got the opportunity to *tell the truth* or even tell my version of events when we were in court, as it wasn't me who was required to take the stand.

Because my ex-husband was the plaintiff in our divorce case, he *was* required to tell the truth and although he may have told the truth in court, he certainly left out a few details. Plus, when he should have been telling the truth to me during the last couple of years of our marriage, he had not. According to him (and the court), our marriage was being dissolved due to "irreconcilable differences." It was a mutual, amicable decision because we had "just grown apart."

That was not my truth. My truth was I was scared, still in love with my husband and thought he was hurting and needed my protection. I was about to learn more than I wanted to know.

This is how *Becoming Unmarried* came about. It started as a journal project in therapy and became the outlet for telling my story. I call what I have put on these pages a narrative non-fiction. It is my version of the events that occurred between May in the year of our marriage's demise and the following January; but what is contained in this book is the truth. In fact, much of what you read here was documented for my legal team in case we needed to use it during the various legal proceedings.

In relaying my *Becoming Unmarried* story—I share my experiences, mistakes and a-ha moments. I have remained as truthful and honest as possible and I hope what I have learned in this process will help you survive your situation. What you are going through may not be the same as what I experienced, but there may be similarities or situations you can use to move yourself through your own divorce process.

In this book, I share what I went through as I navigated my divorce. From learning how to understand lawyers, to discovering my former husband was now starring in some warped version of the sci-fi film *Invasion of the Body Snatchers*. And through all of this, I discovered what kind of woman I really was and what mattered most to me.

I hope each section of this book will help you navigate your own divorce as I offer tips on how to do so with grace—and even a little humor.

I am not a lawyer, a therapist or even an advice professional. I am just in retail marketing. Consider this my legal disclaimer.

To begin, here are a few things you need to keep in mind as you *Become Unmarried*:

- All divorces are different;
- No divorce is easy;
- You are stronger than you realize; and finally,
- You will get through this!

# My Story

May 1st started out like any other Wednesday. The alarm went off at 5:50 AM and S. and I got ready to go to work. We both worked in the same office building, so we had a pretty easy morning routine of getting ready for our half-hour commute into work. Toward the end of the morning, I asked S. about plans we had made for later in the week. He was short with me, which was not a normal response for him. I asked if there was something wrong, and he said, "We can talk about it later today." I didn't think anything of it at the time, as I knew he was having challenges with his boss at work, so our day went on as normal.

After work, while we were in the car heading home, he said, "I guess you want to know what has been bothering me lately."

"I didn't know there was anything bothering you. It's just you got a little short with me this morning, which isn't like you at all," I said. "I know things at work aren't the best for you right now, but I didn't think it was bothering you this much." I reassured him whatever was going on at work; I understood and would make sure his home life was as stress free as possible. "Home will be your sanctuary." I remember telling him.

"Well," he said, "it's not work." He paused. "I don't think I love you anymore and I want out of our marriage." His eyes remained set on the road and he never even looked at me as he continued to drive us home.

For me, May 1st would now always be my "date which will live on in infamy!" to use the words of a former U.S. President. I don't mean to compare the destruction of my marriage to one of the darkest days in our country's history, the bombing of Pearl Harbor, but I do know the conversation that afternoon was as surprising and devastating for me on a personal level. I had no idea it was coming and no immediate way to respond. I was blindsided and from that second on, my marriage of twenty-three years, along with my belief in what marriage was supposed to be, were blown out of the water.

It took several minutes for me to process what S. had just said. Once we got home, he drove the car into the garage, grabbed the keys out of the ignition, got out of the car and went inside the house. Instead of following him, I sat in the car while the waves of confusion and pain washed over me. He didn't seem at all phased by what had just transpired. In fact, he did not come back out to check on me or talk about it any further. He stayed inside while I sat in the car and sobbed. When I finally collected myself enough to get out of the car and stumble into the kitchen, I found him leaning against the counter. He would not make eye contact with me, nor would he say anything.

"What is going on?" I asked, still trying to control my crying.

"I'm not happy anymore and I don't think I love you," he said, looking at me.

"Why?" I asked. "What did I do?"

"It's not you. It's me." That infamous statement was his response.

I continued with questions in rapid succession, as I didn't want to lose this opportunity to get answers.

"How is it not me, if you aren't happy? How long have you felt this way? Is there someone else? What do you mean by not happy? What can I do to help you?"

When he wouldn't give any definitive answers to my questions, I started pleading.

"Please don't do this. I love you so much – you're the only man I have ever loved. What about our families? We've been together almost twenty-six years. You can't just leave me. We can fix this; I know we can. PLEASE – just tell me what is going on!"

As ridiculous as it sounded to me, I had turned into *That Wife*. The Wife who thought she was blissfully married to the perfect man. The Wife who suddenly, randomly discovers she was living in a fairy-tale of her own making. I was her.

# About Me

I grew up in a small town in West Michigan, and with that came many small-town labels: blue-collar, hardworking, Christian-based upbringing, well known and well liked in the community, etc. My parents have been married for over 50 years. My mom is a retired elementary school teacher and daddy is a retired builder. Together, they raised two well-adjusted girls with a lot of love; and as we always joked, a healthy dose of paranoia. My dad made sure his girls were independent, yet leery of others who might try to take advantage of us. Mom made sure we were strong, well-rounded young women who could think for and take care of, ourselves.

I was eighteen years old when I met S. We both worked at the local supercenter while we were going to college. I worked in the shoe department, while he worked in the neighboring paint and hardware department. We didn't really start dating as much as we just started to hang out with everyone from work. There was a large group of us who would catch a bite to eat after our shifts, or maybe go to the movies. We hung out this way for a couple months before he asked me out on our first real date. He took me to his hometown for dinner and a minor-league hockey game with his sister and her husband, as well as their good friend and his wife.

Our first date was a hockey game, and I became hooked on hockey and S. Luckily, I still like hockey.

My ex-husband was twenty-two years old when we started dating, which was a problem for my parents, since to them I was dating a much older guy. A problem, at least until I brought him home to meet my family. My mom had always wanted a son, and I think S. was what my mom would have wanted in her own son. My parents liked him straight away. By the time we had been dating a few months, he was already considered one of the family, something that became evident one particular day.

My parents had new carpeting installed in our living room when S. and I were dating. Dad, my sister and I were strictly forbidden from eating or drinking anything in the room with the new carpeting, lest we want to incur the Wrath of Mom. One day when S. came over after work, he made himself a snack, which he then took into the living room to eat – over the new carpeting. Not a peep from mom. When my sister and I, who had been watching the whole situation transpire, tried to point out he was eating and drinking over her brand-new carpeting, mom just said, "I know I can trust him not to make a mess." My sister and I looked at each other, stunned. I guess we knew who mom's favorite was.

My former husband and I were engaged a year and a half after we started dating. His proposal explained exactly the kind of man I was preparing to spend the rest of my life with. He was not a romantic kind of guy and I knew that going in. He treated me well, but he was practical and very frugal. Since we had been talking about getting married, and he had no idea what kind of engagement ring I wanted, he asked if I wanted to go look at rings. I was excited thinking this was the next big step in our relationship, and was glad he wanted to include me in picking out my engagement ring.

I told him I didn't want anything fancy, just a solitary diamond in a gold band would be fine. Nothing too big, either. We were both still attending college, so we needed to be mindful of money.

One Saturday afternoon, we decided to browse some of the jewelry stores at the mall. In the first store, I found an engagement ring I really liked. It was about a half carat on a gold band. I asked the salesman behind the counter if I could try it on. It looked beautiful on my finger and even fit.

"This would be the kind of ring I would like to have," I said to S.

"So you like this one?" He examined the ring on my finger.

"Yes, this one is very nice," I said.

I started to take the ring off and give it back to the salesman, when S. reached in his back pocket, and out came the checkbook.

"Are you sure you don't want to come back and buy it later?" the salesman stammered.

"If this is the one she wants, I'll just buy it now," he said, writing out the check.

I left the jewelry store at the mall wearing my new diamond engagement ring, which S. had paid for as I stood at the counter.

As we sat in his Ford® Escort in the parking lot after we left the mall, he took the engagement ring off my finger, asked me to marry him and when I said yes, placed the ring back on my hand. I thought his proposal was sweet because it was different and very typical of him, so it seemed the perfect way to get engaged.

I also believed I had the perfect marriage. S. was not hurtful, he never abused me and he took care of me when it came to planning for our future. I thought we could talk about anything and I tried to be very supportive in any decisions he made for us. He was not one for romance and never swept me off my feet. In fact, the only holiday we celebrated with gifts was Christmas. Those special days other couples celebrated together, he considered Hallmark Holidays, something to celebrate so businesses could make money. I guessed that reasoning came from so many years spent working in retail. He said it wasn't necessary to celebrate those days because he loved me every day, not just on special occasions. I bought into it; thinking it was a different and refreshing way to look at our relationship. At the time, I didn't realize we should have been celebrating some of those holidays to show he really cared about me – especially days like our anniversary and my birthday.

# My Situation

During the couple of weeks between the fateful first day of May and the day S. left our home to go live with his parents, I begged him to try counseling. I believed there had to be something beyond his unhappiness in our marriage and if we could just talk about it, we'd discover what that was, fix it and be fine.

After a few days of my pushing for counseling, S. told me I was right and our twenty-six years together were a big investment, too big to just walk away from. He also said we couldn't do this to our families. He offered to help look for counselors and find things we could do together to reconnect. We would make sure we set aside time every day to talk about us – not work, not our families – just us.

I was ELATED! At that moment, you could have told me the world was going to blow up tomorrow and I wouldn't have cared. S. and J were going to BE OK and that was all that mattered. He did love me and we were going to fix this. Couples went through things like this all the time and some put in the hard work to come out stronger for it. That was going to be the case with S. and me. I just knew it. We would grow old together. We would have our happy future. We would BE OK.

Less than 24 hours after S. told me we were going to be OK, he sat me down on the couch and said, "I was wrong. This can't be fixed. I'm going to file for divorce and move in with my mom and dad for a while." My short-lived happiness returned to sadness. As soon as I started to say something, he turned away and got up from the couch. That was it. He didn't say anything else. I sat there in a state of shock as I watched him move some of my things from our bedroom into the spare room, where I would be sleeping for a while.

I sat on the couch and cried; a deep, inconsolable sobbing. Not even a full day had passed since he had agreed to work things out. What could have happened in the last day to change everything? Was there more to this situation than him not loving me and just wanting out of our marriage?

During my sobbing, S. moved my pillows, alarm clock and bedside books into the spare room. I couldn't even muster up enough strength to ask him why I was the one who had to move out of our bedroom. Why wasn't he moving into the spare room? He was the one who wanted out, yet he was moving me into the room where guests stayed. It felt like he was trying to make me feel like the outsider, and I let him do it.

Something was definitely wrong here (duh!). Even though I didn't want to acknowledge this could be the end of our marriage, I put aside trying to think of ways to fix our situation and became curious as to what he was or could be doing. What would cause him to decide NOT to want to fix this? Less than a day ago he was ready to work on our marriage and now he was more determined than before to leave. What had changed?

As a writer and marketing professional, I was pretty good at studying and doing research. I did these things every day in my job and in developing characters for stories. In the coming days, as I came out of my stupor, I decided I needed to do some research on my marriage. I started digging.

First up, my cellphone carrier. Our cell phone contract was in my name, and he had a line in my family plan. I got online and downloaded the call history. Sure enough, there was a phone number I didn't recognize with several phone calls between his phone and this new number over the past several months. There were at least 2-3 calls per week, with some lasting over an hour. I tried looking the phone number up online, but couldn't find the owner. Then I did something I would have NEVER done before. S. wasn't very tech-savvy, and he never bothered to password protect his phone. So, when he was away from his phone, I looked through his contacts to match the number to the call history. There she was – a person from our past – calls, texts and Facebook messaging; most happening in the afternoons while he was supposedly working. No wonder he said his workload was so heavy and he was having problems at work. It appeared he was spending a few hours each week chatting with her in the afternoons, while I was working in the same office building only one floor away.

There was more...

One Sunday morning when he was downstairs, his phone was beeping on the kitchen counter. Since I now knew about the strange phone calls and texts, I picked it up and read the screen. It was one of their text exchanges -

S.: Hey, got home around 11:30 and thought maybe I would catch you on here. I miss you, my Doc. Hope you are getting some much needed rest tonight.

Her: Hi S., Hope you had fun last night. Where did you end up going? Miss you....

There it was – in black and white. He even had a pet name for her; something he always said was childish and stupid. I had tried using pet names with him in the past, and he chastised me. Yet he had one for his other woman? I was crushed. I had proof he was seeking attention with someone else - he even said he missed her.

At this point, I could see the phone screen, but it seemed to be zooming in and out as the phone shook in my hands. And even though I was the only one standing in the kitchen, I felt what I thought were arms around my shoulders, supporting me, trying to keep me from falling down. The room was spinning, but I managed to keep my composure long enough to determine I had to confront S. about this.

I called down the stairs and told him his phone was beeping, and it looked like a pretty important message. When he came upstairs, I handed him his phone.

"Who was the message from?" he asked.

"Not sure, you tell me."

He looked down at his phone and then back at me. I had never seen that look on him before. I hadn't seen that look on anyone else before. It didn't even look human, more like a stone statue where the eyes are empty and blank. He didn't say a word as he put the phone in his pocket and went back downstairs. I was stunned.

"What's going on, S.?" I said as I followed him. "Why are you talking to her?" While I was at it, I told him about the cell phone records and what I had discovered in my recent detective work.

"I am not having this conversation with you," he said, pursing his lips. This was his conclusive shutdown statement, and that was it. He was not going to talk about it – not at all.

Since it appeared S. was unwilling to give me the answers I wanted, I continued my research, this time on our bank account and in our internet browser history on our computer. I found unfamiliar restaurant charges, hotel bookings and receipts. When I asked him about those, I got his, "I'm not having this conversation with you," routine again. I discovered this was his "tell." I had caught him in another lie. When I pressed him for more information, all he said was she was a sympathetic ear.

Really? I didn't know you needed hotel rooms just to talk.

My detective work continued. I started to investigate this woman and her family. That's right – *her family*. She was married and had two children. She lived less than two miles from what used to be my happy home. I had my suspicions she had been in my home at some point during their relationship. Because of this belief, there were now rooms in my own house I couldn't even step into without getting sick to my stomach. Luckily none of those rooms were the bathrooms, so I could throw up whenever I found myself caught up thinking about them together and all his lies.

I became very good at investigating – a regular gum-shoe, so to speak. I knew who this other woman was and when she was talking to my husband. I knew their favorite places to meet. I found her husband's name and where he worked. I knew her kids' names, where they went to school and what activities they were involved in. I had her phone number and the address of her happy home. When armed with all of this knowledge, what did I do? Nothing, except document the details; in case I need to give them to my lawyer during the divorce proceedings.

This became the premise for my book, at least the *Grace* part in the title. Given the research I did and the information I uncovered, the fact that I did not unleash some kind of apocalyptic, hellish revenge on my ex, his "Doc," and her entire family, was nothing short of miraculous. I would find out later, through therapy, that wanting revenge is very common and my not unleashing on my former husband was rare.

In talking with women in similar situations, I found some who dealt with their hurt in rather amusing ways. There have been billboards, full-page newspaper ads and flyers posted in the neighborhoods of the offenders. Some contacted the other woman's family and let them know what was going on. These were knee-jerk reactions to help cope with the pain of discovering their husbands had been cheating. Many times these hurt ladies looked back on their actions with regret. I didn't want to do anything I would regret later on - or anything that would send me to jail. So, I handled my situation with as much grace as I could muster, but it took an awful lot of mustering!

Would revenge have solved anything? It may have been a short-term fix, yes. But had I been the one to show the affair to the world, it would have been me everyone wanted to blame for ruining their lives. Even in my pain, I knew fault needed to lie squarely with S. and his "Doc," not with me. The only way any good could come from this situation was to show people I was the better person. I was the one who would rise above and move forward.

If I had unleashed The Furies on both of them, would I have felt better right then? You bet I would have, but only right then. I'm sure the woman who created a huge billboard using pictures of her former husband and his lover with the word CHEATERS stamped across them, felt immense pleasure the first time she drove by the giant proclamation of what her husband did to her. Yet, I wonder how she felt driving by that same billboard after days, weeks or even months. At what point did revenge turn into regret? I never wanted to find out. So I didn't do anything fueled by rage, even though I felt plenty of it.

I wanted to be able to walk away knowing I had made the right decisions and once this was over and I was on my own, I would have no regrets. I wanted to make sure I had left nothing behind and could move forward knowing I was the better person. If there was going to be any guilt, any bad feelings, unresolved issues and fault, those needed to stay with S.

Keeping that in mind, if I told you I didn't peek at the occult section at the bookstore and library, or Google "how to put a hex on someone" once or twice, I would be lying. But I am a firm believer in karma, and S. has some karma of epic proportions headed his way. I have always found comfort in the Wiccan Reed: *Whatever you send forth comes back to you three-fold.* I've made sure whatever I send forth is well-intentioned, thoughtful and caring. I just wish karma was instant, and I didn't have to keep waiting for it happen. When is the next meteor shower? When is Lake Michigan due for a tsunami? Maybe Nature can take care of things for me.

Often I wished I could call up Nathaniel Hawthorne and have him help me devise a way to bring back the Scarlett Letter. I do believe anyone who comes in contact with S. in the future should be given fair warning of his dishonest behavior. The comedian Bill Engvall performs a skit about stupid people in his show. He wants all of them to wear signs so the rest of us know ahead of time what we are getting ourselves into when dealing with these folks. I think liars and cheaters should also be required to wear some sort of warning so we can avoid contact, or at the very least, know what we are getting into.

S. and I had to coexist in the house for about two weeks between when I confronted him about his affair and his actually moving into his parents' house. I'd like to be able to give you details on how and when he moved out, but there really aren't any. I left to visit my parents on Memorial Day early in the morning and that evening when I got home, he and most of his personal items were gone.

# Chapter Two

## I "Got Served"

About three weeks after S. moved out of our marital home, he called me at my work extension and asked if I wanted to have lunch with him. Hearing from him made me happy because I thought he wanted to talk to me about what he was going through. I was so hoping he would tell me he had changed his mind about leaving me. The rest of the morning dragged by as I looked forward to seeing him. When he met me in the lobby, I was cheerful but he was silent and sullen, only acknowledging my presence with an occasional "yeah" or "OK" when I talked to him. I drove, and when we were in the parking lot of the restaurant, I noticed he had brought a folder with him.

"What's that?" I asked.

"We can talk about it after we eat," he said.

As we ate lunch and I babbled on about being glad to see him since I wanted things to go back to the way they were—with us together. I think I even remember telling him how alone I felt in the house, and I missed him.

He didn't say much during lunch, and when we were back in the parking lot, he handed me the folder. I asked him what it was, and he didn't say anything, so I opened it. Inside were very legal looking documents and I didn't have to read past the first few lines to see they were divorce papers. He was serving those papers to me personally.

Remember how S. had proposed to me while we were in his Ford Escort in the parking lot of the mall? Well, now we were becoming unmarried in my Ford Ranger in the parking lot of a restaurant. Talk about irony.

In sharing this story with fellow divorcees, I discovered most people received their divorce papers in the mail, or a process server delivered them. S. believed hand-delivering the papers would be more personal, and told me he didn't want me to be uncomfortable because a stranger had delivered them. He was only trying to make it easier on me. Right. I guess I should have appreciated that my soon to be ex-husband was just looking out for me. He was so concerned, you know. According to him, I needed to sign the papers right then and there so he could start the process with the lawyer he had chosen to represent our case.

When I asked if I could take them home to look over, he told me to just sign them. I shouldn't worry since these papers didn't contain much information. They were just a formality to get the process started. Since I was still at the *trusting phase* of all this, I signed the papers, closed the folder and handed it back to him.

"We should probably get back to the office now," he said. "I have a 1:00 meeting."

Even though I was pretty much in shock, I managed to put the truck into gear and drove us back to the office. I must admit there were some warning bells going off in my head. Maybe I was starting to come around, after all.

# One Lawyer or Two?

S. told me he had hired one attorney to represent both of us. However, when I went looking for my own lawyer, I found out hiring one lawyer for both parties isn't recommended. In a divorce matter, a lawyer can only represent one of the parties. Otherwise there is a conflict of interest. This brings me to a key point—no matter what anyone tells you; you need to hire your own lawyer.

Before S. moved out and I discovered all the *bad things* about my former husband, he explained how the mediation process would work, stressing that by using only one lawyer, we would save money and the process would not take as long. We didn't have any children; we didn't have debt and it would be easier if we had one lawyer to oversee the process.

He continued this explanation while we sat together at the dining room table one evening. He got out a piece of paper to show me how everything would be divided in the mediation and if we kept things simple, we wouldn't have to go to court. Since Michigan is a no-fault divorce state, he explained we would split everything 50/50. On the piece of paper, he wrote down what I understood to be our assets—a figure for our cash, a rough estimate of our 401K plans, and other numbers representing the equity in our properties and various household assets.

He explained how I would receive half the equity in the properties we owned, half the cash, and half the total value of our 401K plans. It was as simple as a 50/50 split. And since we wouldn't have to worry about two lawyers, our divorce would be easy and it wouldn't be costly.

According to him, everything would take place in the lawyer's office and then she would submit our agreement to the court. I nodded my head, thinking I was luckier than a lot of women in my place since S. was going to handle everything and make sure I was set for the future.

Was I crazy? Too trusting? Maybe. I just couldn't bring myself to believe S. would do anything else to hurt me. I would discover later, mediation with one lawyer would have allowed him to control everything about our divorce from start to finish. I believe control was the *real* reason he wanted to avoid going to court, not my supposed well-being.

When I think back to that dining room table conversation, I was fully ready to move forward with the single lawyer mediation process. Even though my family told me to get my own lawyer; my friends told me I needed my own lawyer; and everyone I talked to who had been through a divorce told me to get a good lawyer. I wasn't listening. I was convinced S. was right. When it came to our finances and our future, he had always been right. Why would he lead me down the wrong path now? Because he was only looking out for himself, that's why. Wrapping my head around the fact he didn't seem to care about my future and finally giving in to the truth was difficult. It was inconceivable to think after all the years we had been together he no longer cared about me. However, to appease the chorus of worrywarts who wanted me to get my own lawyer, I followed through with a couple of free consultations with divorce attorneys. These individuals were either recommended to me or ones I found through research on the internet. Two were phone consultations and a couple were in person. Every lawyer I spoke with said the same thing—you don't have to hire me, but you MUST get yourself a lawyer.

One of the lawyers explained that S. was incorrect in telling me a single lawyer could handle the mediation process. It was an ethical violation for one lawyer to represent both parties in a divorce. She stated she had seen this behavior before in people who were attempting to take advantage of their significant other during the divorce process. Since she was the most informative lawyer, and was thorough in explaining the process to me, she was the one I hired. Plus, she reminded me of Carrie Fisher (yep, Princess Leia), whom I greatly admired. My lawyer had a quick wit and honest empathy for my situation. Later, I would discover she could be a pit-bull, too, which was an added benefit in the courtroom.

I'll say it again; make sure you hire your own attorney to represent you in the divorce process. Also, don't wait until you actually get served with divorce papers. I found out from my new lawyer I should not have signed any divorce documents without having a legal team look through them first. Because I did sign them before a lawyer could recommend a course of action, I wasn't given the opportunity to respond on the record to the court that I had discovered, and S. had admitted to, having an affair. I would have to wait to include what I knew in documents prepared for a trial brief later in the process.

Three things you need to consider when picking a divorce lawyer:

1. Choose a lawyer whose office is in the county where you live. This isn't a requirement, but can help save money and time. All court proceedings will be conducted in the county in which you reside. If your lawyer is from outside the county, your legal fees could be higher due to travel expenses and time spent going to and from the courthouse, or he/she may not be familiar with your county's judicial offices, which may put you at a disadvantage.

2. Choose a lawyer you feel comfortable around. The divorce process is detailed, often difficult to understand and the legal terminology is something you are probably not familiar with. Having a lawyer who can explain things to you and make you feel confident with your decisions is definitely a plus.

I had started my college career as a prelaw student and changed to marketing after spending two years trying to decipher legal lingo. I didn't enjoy trying to understand the documents back then, and I didn't want to try to learn it again. I relied on my lawyer to guide me through the paperwork. And there was *a lot* of paperwork, which we will cover later in the book.

3. Hire a lawyer <u>before</u> you sign the divorce papers or anything else your soon-to-be ex-spouse puts in front of you. Have your lawyer review before you put your signature on anything.

# Setting Your Divorce Strategy

Throughout the divorce process, I often felt I was receiving too much information from too many sources to make smart decisions on how to move forward. I knew I had to make the *right* choices. Often I felt rushed and didn't know if I had enough time to think things through and make the best choice for me.

As a marketer, I kept reminding myself to stick to the basics. My colleagues and I call sticking with the basic principles *Marketing 101*, when we set our marketing strategies and put together campaigns. I followed the same process when I set my divorce strategy.

Between my first and second court dates, I took a step back, sat down with a notebook and got back to basics by setting my divorce strategy. We'll call it my *Becoming Unmarried Marketing Campaign*, and this was how I applied it to my situation.

### Becoming Unmarried Marketing Campaign

1. Define my objectives.
   a. Ensure my financial future was secure.
   b. Determine the actual status and size of our marital estate.

2. What were the hurdles to fulfilling those objectives?
   a. Lack of information from my former husband regarding what was available.
3. Determine the steps to get to my objectives.
   a. Hire a good lawyer.
   b. Talk to financial advisors.
4. Evaluate and measure my progress toward reaching my goals.
5. Adjust steps accordingly to stay on track.
6. CELEBRATE SUCCESS!!!

My number one objective was to make sure my future was secure. This may not be your objective, so think about your priorities. You may have your own physical safety or the safety of your children to consider as your primary objective.

Set your objectives, write them down and keep reviewing them. You may discover your objectives change part-way through your divorce process. If you adjust your objectives, you may also need to adjust the Becoming Unmarried Marketing Campaign so you stay the course.

S. appeared at our first court proceeding with inaccurate asset documentation. Therefore, I needed to make sure he wasn't hiding money or lying about what we actually owned in our investment accounts. My first course of action was asking my lawyer to help hire the resources I would need to make sure we accounted for *every dollar*. I talked to numerous financial advisors and accountants to see what recourse I had for finding any hidden money. After gathering those details, I was confident my legal team and I could account for just about everything in our martial estate. Could S. have been skimming cash out of our accounts in small amounts and hiding it in coffee cans in the backyard? He could have, but by carefully reviewing the numbers with my advisors, I felt comfortable with everything we documented and assigned value to for the marital estate. Still, those dollars totaled more than what S. and his legal team had originally provided to the courts. Much more. It was important to verify the real dollars to be divided during the divorce so I could receive half of what was actually documented in our estate, not half of what my former husband was willing to share.

Throughout the divorce process, I kept tabs on where I was in meeting my objectives. As I kept my financial future in sight, there were a few times when I wanted to stop paying people to help me. Paying the lawyer to follow up with financial advisors and retirement associates was expensive. Making multiple appointments with those same advisors was time consuming and took me away from work. However, in the end, I made the right choices because I signed a divorce document that allowed me to purchase property for my new home and write a book I hope, will help other women meet their Becoming Unmarried objectives, too.

Given the circumstances and the nature of divorce in general, I would deem my *Becoming Unmarried Marketing Campaign* a success. If you stay the course and do the work, your campaign will be successful, as well!

# Let the Games Begin!

The divorce process was not easy. To be honest, it sucked. It was time consuming, difficult to understand, and when it began, it was a soul crushing defeat.

It felt adversarial and competitive. I could see a glimpse of what kind of game I was in for on the first lines of the papers when S. served them to me. They said:

Plaintiff (him)
**vs**.
Defendant (me)

Vs. stands for versus, which is Latin for against. Him against me. Just like a sporting event, divorce was a competition, and not a friendly one. There would be one winner and one loser. I, just like you, needed to decide which one to be.

S. had always been very competitive. He played high school football and throughout our marriage, he played hockey, golf and other sports. In this new game he had signed us up for, I knew he was not about to lose. He wouldn't even allow me to gain an advantage on the playing field, so to speak. In fact, every time I thought I was gaining, or at least holding my own, I would get knocked down by yet another motion from his lawyer or a problem with his documentation discovered by my lawyer. The volleys went back and forth until I felt as though I was totally defeated.

This chapter is intended to cover some of the things you may encounter during the legal process. It will give you pointers on how to remain cool, calm and collected; and make sure you end up finishing the game with the win.

# Learning the Lingo

During my short stint as a pre-law college student, one of the books I bought was the *Black's Law Dictionary*, the leading reference guide for legal definitions and terminology. I didn't use it much during my pre-law days, but I sure used it a lot during my divorce. I read every document my lawyer sent me to make sure I understood what it said. It wasn't that my lawyer wasn't explaining everything to me, but after what my ex-husband was putting me through, I had a hard time believing anything *anyone* told me. I was not about to take anything at face value, no matter who was giving me the information.

I learned legal copy was nothing like marketing copy. For clarification, *copy* is a marketing term for text, or the words on a page. Legal copy was cold, unemotional and antiquated. Some of the words were so old I swear cobwebs would form on the page as I read them. For example, you will see words like *hereinafter, duly sworn, subpoena, affidavit,* and *deposition.* Some of the letters I received from my legal team didn't even say, "Hey, we mailed your papers to the courthouse and the other lawyer today!" No, instead they said the documents had been "deposited in a governmental mail receptacle the enclosed, sealed envelopes plainly addressed with postage thereon fully prepaid."

Good heavens. No wonder it took me three times longer to read and decipher all the correspondence I received from my legal team. Why couldn't they just speak plain English? Actually, they were, just not a version of English we deal with every day.

Remember, if you have any questions about documents you receive, you should schedule a meeting with your lawyer. At the very least, call her to review the documents so you understand their intent. Don't assume everything makes sense and you are good to go. One vague or misplaced word could leave you vulnerable. If you have a close friend who has been through a similar situation, ask if she would be willing to sit down with you and go through some of her old divorce papers. This will give you an idea of what the terminology looks like and what will be contained in the briefs. Oops – I'd better define this, too. A brief is a document that outlines or summarizes the status of your case for the courts. There will be a few of these filed by your legal team and the opposing legal team during each stage of the divorce.

The key thing to remember here is you don't know what you don't know—and what you don't know can do some pretty significant damage. Make an effort to stay informed.

# Documentation

In real estate, the catch-phrase is "Location, Location, Location." In divorce, it is "Documentation, Documentation, Documentation!" If you know your former spouse has done or said something that could work toward your advantage in the proceedings, but you have no proof of it—it is no good. Therefore, KEEP EVERY PIECE OF PAPER! All the letters from your lawyer (and there will be a lot of them), bank statements, property titles and bills, along with retirement and financial planning summaries. Your lawyer will give you a list (a *long* list) of everything you need to document. If you are still talking to your soon-to-be former spouse, keep any texts, emails or other forms of communication. Keep voicemails, especially if they are threatening, which happens more often than I realized. If necessary, record any phone calls if you talk to one another. Turn copies of everything over to your lawyer. She will decide what to do with them as you go along. Keep a copy for yourself, and even though I know this sounds a little paranoid, put a third copy of everything someplace you are guaranteed he cannot gain access. In my case, it was at my parent's house.

Let me take a step back here... Why did I keep *three* copies of everything? Because most of the divorce process was going on while I was living at *the marital estate.* S. still had access to the house and I couldn't be sure he wasn't going through everything while he was there. It seemed he would only go to the house to get his things when he was certain I would not be there. To be safe, I kept back-up copies at my parents' house.

# Your Day (maybe many) in Court

## Getting Ready for Your Court Date

Once I hired my lawyer and she responded to my former husband's attorney, it was about two weeks before I got my first summons to appear in court. When I received the summons, two things hit me hard. One, this divorce thing was really happening. Two, why did these pieces of paper make me feel like I was a criminal? To see the word Defendant after my name on the summons made me think, *Am I criminal? What did I do wrong? Why am I being singled out?* The word Defendant also made one thing absolutely clear—I needed to defend myself. I had taken the first step by hiring a great lawyer; but that was only the beginning. Now it was time to be diligent and thorough (crazy & paranoid, according to my former husband), to make sure I was not being taken advantage of during the divorce proceedings. It was time to roll-up my sleeves and put in the work of making sure my future was secure.

Your lawyer should send you information regarding your first day in court. It will list the time, date and location for your hearing. Memorize it, as being late or missing it could put you in bad standing with the judge, which is not where you want to be during your very first appearance.

In order to make sure you are prepared for your first day in court, schedule a meeting with your lawyer, or talk to people who have been through the process. I learned presenting yourself to the court is very much like a business meeting, so I could fall back on my work experiences. I am not afraid of appearing in front of people as I have given presentations to groups of all sizes. I have been involved with creative reviews with clients, large presentations for marketing planning, and campaign updates with executives. Presentations and speeches don't intimidate me. Yet, the thought of going to court and facing a judge terrified me. I didn't know what to expect. I wanted to make sure I was well prepared, so I met with my lawyer to go through what my day in court would be like.

I tend to over-prepare for everything. Ask anyone who has gone on road trips or vacations with me. When planning itineraries, I research everything we will be doing on the trip. Places to stay, eat, visit, shop—everything. I book activities in advance, and print out nice little packets of information for everyone, so no one feels left behind or out of the loop. Like I said—over-prepared for everything.

My pre-trial visit with my legal team was no exception. I showed up for the meeting with a four-inch binder containing copies of every piece of paper I had received so far. Seeing my big binder, my lawyer laughed a little. By this time, she had known me for a few months and was aware of my hypersensitivity to the whole process. In addition to my binder, I had a list of questions for her to help me prepare for the first court appearance:

- What does the courtroom look like – is it like Law & Order?
- Will the judge address me directly? What will he ask me? How do I respond?
- How long will it take?
- Will I have to see *him*?
- Do I have to talk to him or his lawyer?
- Will it all be over when we leave the court house?

She appeared to understand I was scared I was missing something and if I left any stone unturned or left any open vulnerabilities; I believed S. would use those opportunities to his advantage.

Because I was nervous S. hadn't reported all our finances correctly, based on the pre-trial brief we had seen from his lawyer, my attorney was prepared to ask the court for an adjournment of our case to set a new trial date. This would allow us more time for due diligence in researching my finances. This meant the first court appearance would not last very long, and my lawyer would do all the talking.

Even though I had my big list of questions and was ready to go, it looked as though our first hearing would be one where we asked for more time and set another court date. My attorney indicated this was pretty common in divorce proceedings, since not many couples were ready to agree on everything the first time out. Still, I asked her to explain more of the process to me so I would be ready to go next time.

# Court Date - Round One

I learned a lot at my first court date, and here are some pointers.

## Arrive early

Arrive at the courthouse a minimum of 15 minutes early, especially if you live in a city or county with busy courthouses. Everyone must pass through a security check similar to airport security. So, arrive in plenty of time, especially if you are carrying a big binder that needs to be scanned through the x-ray machine.

Family Court divorce proceedings are almost like little factories. After you have gone through security, the first thing you want to look for is the schedule for each of the judges, which informs you of your courtroom and time. You may notice other people waiting for their court appearances mulling about in the hallways and lobbies of the courthouse. There may also be people sitting in the courtroom itself, waiting for the judge to hear their case. The cases are scheduled to last about 15 to 20 minutes, so there is an assembly line of people waiting to go before the judge.

## Dress Appropriately

Let's hope Emily Post never has to go to court, as I believe she would be appalled by what she sees in the way of attire. Now, I admit to being on the conservative side when it comes my appearance. Being a professional who is expected to dress business casual or business professional at the office, I believe jeans and flip-flops are weekend wear. Judging from my visits to the courthouse, not everyone agreed.

My first court date was in mid-September, and normal fashion rules state the color white is not to be worn after Labor Day, much less summer casual clothing. However, if you go by the example set by one young lady at my first court appearance, a tank top, short shorts and strappy sandals are perfectly acceptable any time of the year and in any setting, even when you present yourself to a judge. I told myself I was just getting older, and maybe this was fine by today's standards, but it didn't work. I was still surprised and a bit disappointed.

I was dressed in dress pants and a suit coat. I did wear a bright yellow top, as yellow is my lucky color, but my look overall was professional and serious. I wanted to make sure I appeared to the judge as someone who was respectful of his courtroom and the proceedings. You need to do the same. Dress as though you are attending a job interview in a professional setting. Wear a suit or nice dress, if you can. And you might want to keep the jewelry to a minimum. A lawyer from another case was wearing an armful of bangles. Every time she moved her hands, which was a lot, they rattled throughout the lobby of the courthouse. I didn't get to see her present inside the courtroom, but I couldn't help but wonder if the judge could hear anything above the din of her bracelets.

When it comes to dressing for court—sensible is good. Leave the jeans, tank tops, flip-flops and yoga pants at home.

## Pay Attention

Watching the people in the courthouse was entertaining, but it also shed light on this new situation and setting. By just observing other people while I was waiting for my lawyer, I learned a few things to keep in mind.

Stay close to your lawyer. She'll have a good idea of how things are going and she'll have the court schedule so you will know when you need to be in front of the judge.

Don't stray too far from your assigned courtroom. Like I said before, these proceedings are on a pretty tight schedule. You'll start off on the wrong foot if you keep the judge waiting.

If you do appear before the judge, you may need to address the court, so pay attention to what the judge is saying and who he is addressing. Always answer the judge clearly and address him or her as "Your Honor."

As I waited to see the judge, I observed the custody discussion of a young couple. The father requested reduced child support due to his reduced hours at work. Whenever the judge would ask the mother how much support she required per child, the father made snorting noises and leaned way back in his chair. Each time, the judge would look up over his glasses and ask the young man if he needed a glass of water. It appeared the father had not been forthcoming with information regarding his work history and his wages when his hours were reduced. To make matters worse, he mumbled a lot. After about 15 minutes, the judge ruled the young man would not receive a reduction on his child support because he couldn't account for his lost hours. I couldn't help but wonder if his conduct in the courtroom had something to do with the judge's decision.

It's OK to be nervous, apprehensive and even scared. Just try to keep it under control. I became overwhelmed, even though I had my parents and my sister there to support me. It was crowded, busy and noisy. When I saw S. in the lobby talking with his lawyer, he looked so normal, calm and collected. That only added to my anxiety. S and his lawyer were smiling and laughing. Yet I felt as though he was ripping my life to shreds. *Quit looking at him!* I told myself, but it was too late. Tears burned in my eyes, my heart began beating harder and I found it hard to breathe. I didn't want him to see my panic. When looked at my lawyer, she could see I was in distress. She shuttled me off to one of the empty conference rooms and told me to relax. She said she would take care of things, for me to stay put. Then she disappeared.

I sat in the conference room alone and collected myself for what seemed like an eternity, even though it was only a few minutes. Our case was scheduled for 1:00 PM and even though it was now 1:05, I could see the judge was still handling another case. After another 10 minutes or so, my lawyer came back into the room. She had talked with my ex-husband's lawyer and the conversation had not been helpful. S. and his lawyer had prepared their trial brief, but not provided any actual back up documents for the marital assets. The brief had nice, round numbers for all our assets; from the bank accounts to the retirement funds, and even the value of our house. Everything ended in a nice, neat zero. My lawyer and I had actual copies of EVERYTHING, two sets of documents, even. One set showed the values of everything during June (when S. first filed for divorce), and another set showed the values of everything current to the day prior to our court proceedings. There was over a 20% difference between the trial brief prepared by my ex's team and our brief. His showed a *much lower* value. My lawyer then sought an aside with the judge, which meant the two lawyers would meet with the judge in chambers to decide next steps. I remained in the conference room.

More waiting, except now, instead of feeling like I wanted to curl into a ball and cry, I was fuming. S. was trying to cheat me out of my fair share of the settlement—again! I thought back to the dining room table conversation where he explained the process and how I would be entitled to half of our assets. Apparently, he wanted me to have half of what he said was there, not half of what was documented. This time though, I had my lawyer and she was not going to let S. or his legal team get away with inaccuracies.

My lawyer was smiling when she returned from the meeting with the judge, which I took as a good sign. The judge was not happy with the discrepancies and was especially displeased with the lack of actual documentation to back up the values my ex-husband's legal team had put into their trial brief. The judge granted a 60-day adjournment; and both lawyers were instructed to use the spreadsheet and documentation my lawyer and I had prepared as the actual, recorded values for the division of assets. I asked her if this was considered a win, and she said yes.

My parents and sister were sitting in the lobby when I came out of the conference room and told them the news. They said while I was sitting in the conference room, S. appeared to get chastised by his lawyer for not reporting the proper values on everything from the house appraisals to our actual cash on hand. My parents and sister overheard his lawyer asking questions like "Why didn't you tell me how much cash you had?" and "Why didn't you send me the statements?" All he did was shrug, and stare at the copy of our spreadsheet in his hand.

I avoided having to be in the same space as my former husband when we left the courthouse. This time it wasn't because I didn't want him to see me crying, though. Now it was because the courthouse was attached to the county jail and there were a lot of police officers on duty. I figured it would be too easy for me to get arrested if he should happen to "fall" down the front stairs.

# Court Date - Round Two

Sixty days later (November), we had what I thought would be our final court date. My lawyer and I had spent the previous two months gathering more information on how much the marital estate was worth. We had hired a third-party valuation company to assess the value of my  ex-husband and my retirement packages now and in the future. We also made sure we had accurately documented the values of everything my former husband and I owned, right down to the household items to be divided.

I used the two months to think about where I wanted to be in my new future. Financially and emotionally, I had big decisions to make.

Because S. had been earning a company-provided pension by his employer the entire time we were married, he was entitled to a pension upon his retirement. I had to decide if I wanted him to pay me the amount it would be worth today as a lump sum, or if I wanted to make a portion of his pension a part of my own retirement plan by receiving a pension check each month when he started to collect. The 'pay me now' dollar amount was significant enough to be a nice down payment on a house of my very own. However, in the end I decided to take the part I was entitled to as part of my retirement planning. I knew if I was smart with my money over the next several years, the monthly amount would be a nice addition to the 401Ks and other investments I now had in place.

I knew a large cash payment would have created a financial hardship for him. He was getting both of the homes we owned, which also meant taking on those mortgages. Let me be clear; not asking for the lump sum payment was not to protect him; I just decided I needed to look out for my long-term future.

One of the most difficult decisions I had to make throughout this whole process was to determine if I wanted to try to recoup any money S. had spent on his affair. I would need to research how much money he had used, and determine if I wanted to spend time and resources going after it. I really wanted his affair to be a part of the court proceedings. Maybe by telling the judge S. had spent some of MY hard-earned money on another woman; it would force him to own his behavior. However, after reviewing bank statements and receipts, my legal team and I determined it was going to cost more money to investigate those funds than I would be able collect. Reluctantly, I let the monetary proof of the affair go.

I did not document everything I knew about his affair with the court. We did include the statement of his affair with a married woman in our trial brief, but we didn't include her name or contact information. I was trying to take the higher road even though I did want to bring some of his horrible decisions to light. I wanted him to be exposed for the liar he had become. He didn't seem to take ownership of what he had done, and I wanted accountability, which appeared to be something he didn't possess in many aspects of his life.

One day, earlier in the divorce proceedings, S. had been over helping with yard work. There were a few bills to be paid, so he went to the basement office so he could gather the bills and take them back to his parents' condo. I followed him down the stairs.

"I'm thinking about naming your girlfriend in the court documents," I said.

"Whatever," he said with his back to me. "That's your decision." We entered the office and he sat down at the desk, still not looking at me.

"You're OK with ruining another family?"

"Whatever happens between her and her family is her problem, not mine." He grabbed the bills from the desk organizer, stood and started past me to go back upstairs.

"Really? So you have no fault here?"

"Not with her family," he said. "Besides, she can't do anything about her situation for a while, at least not until her kids are older."

With that, he walked back up the stairs and out the door.

I was stunned. I knew he didn't end his contact with her during our divorce proceedings and now it seemed he didn't care about her any more than he cared about me. Did he just want to have an affair because he knew it would do irreparable harm to our marriage? Something I would not be able to forgive him for? Maybe he thought it would allow him to walk away without any responsibility.

I finally determined going into detail about the affair was futile and not worth the time and money. It was still going to be up to my legal team to make sure everything was accurately accounted for, which was a better use for my resources. After we had gathered all our documentation, we sent copies of everything to the other lawyer. I found it ironic, as during our marriage, S. had controlled our finances. Finding investments, calculating costs and savings, was almost an obsession for him. Yet now it was up to *me* to provide accurate financial information to the court.

I handled Court Date - Round Two much better than the first. This time we went in front of the judge and my ex-husband's lawyer did most of the presenting, while the judge reviewed the numbers my lawyer and I had presented. S. and I both had to answer questions stating we were aware of why we were in court, that our lawyers had explained the process and possible outcomes to us and we were comfortable with our representation and dividing of our assets. They asked us to verify we had no minor children or child support/custody needs. The court even asked me if I was currently pregnant no less than five times. Five times!!! I answered no each time, but when the judge asked me the fifth time, I wanted to stand up and shout, "Look, I am not pregnant! He's screwing somebody else. Maybe you need to ask his girlfriend this question!" But I didn't. I just looked at the judge and said, "No, Your Honor, I am not pregnant."

Later I discovered the pregnancy question gets asked during all divorce proceedings and is meant to cover two things. One, to make sure there wasn't an unborn child needing consideration in a custody hearing; and two, because in the state of Michigan, a child who was the result of an extra-marital affair will be considered a product of the mother's *existing* marriage. I understood the court's need to be sure I wasn't pregnant, but I still found the repeated questioning annoying.

After the attorneys presented the case to the judge and he reviewed how the assets were being divided, the only thing left was to finalize the divorce. We decided the divorce would take effect on January 1, so we could still file taxes jointly as a couple that year, which would save us both money.

At the end of the proceedings, the judge addressed me stating he needed to verify the declaration of the divorce with the plaintiff, and I was free to go. My lawyer had told me before the hearing this was the last step, and I could stay or leave. I knew S. was going to be asked if this was his decision, that he initiated the process, and he was convinced our marriage could not be repaired. As he prepared to take the stand, my lawyer leaned over and asked me if I wanted to leave.

"Not a chance," I said. I wanted to hear my almost officially ex-husband answer the judge. I wanted him to OWN this. It was hard to listen to him say he wanted to be granted a divorce, and harder still to hear the judge say he could have his divorce. Yet, the worst part was he would not acknowledge my presence in the courtroom. There was no eye contact at all while he was on the stand or as he walked back to his chair.

If I had to do it again, I'm not sure I would stay to hear the declaration. I was hoping he would show some remorse. I thought maybe he'd look at me and say, "Tami, I am so sorry to put you through this. Please forgive me and my selfishness." I was looking for *something*, some emotion for what he was putting me through. Nothing happened. In fact, there must have been a pretty interesting scratch or stain on the podium, as he spent his time looking down very intently and never even glanced in my direction.

After the hearing was over, I spent a couple of minutes in the lobby asking my lawyer about our next steps. She told me the other legal team would be responsible for drafting the final divorce documents based on what had transpired in the courtroom. We would review those documents, sign and return them to be filed with the court. Once we had signed the final documents, there would be quit claim deeds for our two houses to be filed. My lawyer and I would be responsible for the QDROs (Qualified Domestic Relations Orders), which were required for processing the retirement funds. She indicated we should have our final paperwork filed by January 1, which was my belief as I left the court in November. What transpired was quite different, so I would learn in a couple of months.

Since every phone call or email to my lawyer resulted in some sort of fee, I had to adjust my mentality of always needing to know what was going on with my case. Knowing we were close to the end, with only a few minor paperwork details to be tidied up, I didn't call my lawyer until mid-December. When I did call, she indicated she had seen the draft of the final judgment but it didn't quite match the transcripts from our final court hearing, so she sent revisions to my former husband's attorney. Since the changes we were requesting matched the court proceedings, she didn't think it would take too long for the final approvals. We should still be set by January 1.

The Holidays came and went. On January 2, I called my lawyer again. She still hadn't heard anything from the other lawyer. By now, I was annoyed. S. wanted this divorce, so why was he holding things up? Was he still trying to take advantage of me?

On January 9th, I finally heard from my lawyer. She called to let me know she had received a summons to appear in court as we *couldn't agree on the final divorce language*. Another court date? I felt blindsided - again. Why did we have to go back to court? He was saying we didn't agree on the language, yet we *did*. It was his attorney who used language that didn't match the agreements made in court. There were items in the draft both my lawyer and I could tell were boilerplate language (i.e. common legal phrases), and not applicable to our case. There was a paragraph allowing the parties to ask for spousal support in the future if there were debts to settle and we asked his legal team to remove it. We wanted the final order to match what was agreed upon during the November hearing. On multiple occasions during the process, I told S. I wanted any and all mentions of spousal support to be taken out of the divorce documents. We made almost exactly the same amount of money, so there was no need to even mention spousal support. Yet, nearly every time I reviewed briefs, spousal support language was included.

In this new draft, there were entire sections that didn't appear to be applicable to our divorce, and didn't match the court transcripts. My lawyer asked for those paragraphs to be stricken from the final document.

I was angry, and shot a few texts off to my former husband expressing how I felt about him holding up the process and making us go back to court again. He replied by saying it was my fault as all I had to do was sign the agreement, but instead I had to be difficult. I guessed if my not agreeing to verbiage not in the transcripts from the November court date meant we couldn't come to an agreement on the language, then I was indeed the one holding up the case! He obviously needed to lay the blame on me instead of himself.

When I asked how he could just let the documents go and have his attorney file a motion without making sure he really wanted to go to court again, he replied via text, "I didn't read them."

"Then why did you agree to let this go court?" I asked.

"My lawyer told me I had to."

Sigh.
Back to court we went!

My ex-husband didn't even bother to show up at court for the final hearing. Apparently, it was too inconvenient for him to miss work. But I went, as I wanted to make sure the final, *final* documents filed with the court were 100% accurate. My lawyer was already there when I arrived. She had brought the transcripts from our November date to share with the other lawyer. They met in a conference room and my lawyer indicated the verbiage we were asking to be removed was not supposed to be in the final order. My ex-husband's lawyer agreed to the changes on the spot, striking the four paragraphs in question. My lawyer had me initial the changes and sign at the end of the form. Why this discussion couldn't have taken place in one of the law offices, I had no idea.

Not more than 10 minutes later, we went in front of the same judge from the previous hearings. He questioned why we were all gathered here again. When opposing council explained she was willing to change the verbiage to better match the transcripts from our previous hearing, the judge indicated this could have been settled without having to appear in court. He then asked if the plaintiff was there to sign the final order. S.'s lawyer said he was not, but she would take the documents back to her office so he could sign them when it was more convenient. She would then e-file them with the court. The judge told her to sign for him acting as his representative, so the order could be filed immediately and not create further delays.

After nearly eight months, the process was over and I had a copy of the final divorce order. It contained the judge's signature, the lawyers' signatures, my signature and a scribbled set of initials where my ex-husband's signature should have been. Seems like he couldn't even own what he had done with the courts.

# Chapter Three
## School of Hard Knocks

Class was officially in session when S. filed for divorce. I learned some new and scary things about my former husband I wasn't ready to believe. There was no room for denial now. It was time for a crash-course on divorce from the School of Hard Knocks. As a self-proclaimed procrastinator, I tried to ignore the following Hard Lessons and pretend they didn't exist, but I soon learned I had to at least acknowledge what was happening in order to move forward. I'm sharing these insights with you. You may want to start taking notes.

### Hard Lesson #1. This Is Really Happening.

It is not a bad dream, and you can't try to shake it off or run away. I kept hoping I would wake up from the nightmare, or S. would come to his senses and change his mind about leaving me.

While I was still living in the house and S. came over to do yard work, I would ask him if he had changed his mind yet. He always said no, but I thought I should at least keep asking the question. It took a lot of procrastinating, but I finally realized he wasn't going to change his mind. He wanted out of our marriage and was going to keep moving forward with the process. It didn't seem to matter to him that I wanted to try therapy.

**TRUTH**: The sooner you learn he is leaving and there isn't anything you can do about it; the sooner you will be able to gather your wits enough to trudge forward with the process of defending yourself during the divorce.

**Hard Lesson #2. You may not recognize your former husband anymore.**

Alien abduction? Ghostly possession? Demonic imposter? *Invasion of the Body Snatchers*, maybe? These were questions I asked myself when I tried to figure out what was happening to my former husband. He looked like the man I loved. He even sounded like him, but something was different about his entire demeanor. Physically he was S., but his behavior had completely changed. No longer was he the laid-back man who was open with me and told me not to lose my patience over the little things. Now he lost his temper over any question I asked him. He was secretive and denied things he had said or done. Plus, I kept catching him in lies ...a lot of them. It seemed nearly everything he said to me was contradictory. Things that I had wanted to do all along during our marriage were now the reasons he wanted to leave. He told me we had become more like roommates, but when we were together and I wanted to cuddle on the couch or go out for a nice evening together, he would say, "No, we don't do that sort of thing." He told me I was too accommodating. Yet, had I ever asked him to reconsider any of his plans, he would say, "I told you not to tell me what I can and cannot do." I never questioned him or told him no. I was not allowed to use the word 'let' in our marriage, so I didn't. I was the wife who never complained when he hung out with the guys for long weekends or went to high school football games with his brothers on Friday nights in the fall. It wasn't until later I found out some of his outings had turned into dates with another woman.

Now he expected me to be OK with what he had done, let him destroy our marriage and move on. I thought I was doing right by my husband, but I didn't really know who he was, at least not toward the end.

**TRUTH**: Pay attention to who your husband has become and what he is saying and doing. You may think you are doing right by your husband by not questioning him, but you need to realize everything he does now is to protect himself.

### Hard Lesson #3. Conversations may betray you.

Not only should you be cautious about believing what your former husband says to you, there may be times when conversations between the two of you will become so emotional you may not remember what he actually said. Things you say back to him may also betray you during the divorce process.

To help me keep track of our exchanges, I kept a journal. I would write down the time and place of the conversation, and include as many details I could remember about what was said. I included my responses in my journal, too. Although during most of our conversations, S. seemed to know what to say to strike a nerve. Much of what he said hit me so hard I would shut down. S. would then disengage from the conversation and leave. There were times when he didn't just strike a nerve; he cut me to the core. Looking back, I wish I had been more forceful in my responses to him. I wish I wouldn't have shut down or let his words affect me so much that I let him walk away. I wish I had gotten angry at him and his hurtful words, but I couldn't do it. Much of the time, I could not even articulate what I wanted to say to him in response. He always got the final say, because I let him or was too stunned to stop him.

These were some of the more wounding things he said:

"Even if we decided to go to therapy now, would you really want to waste the next three months or six months going to a counselor just to hear me tell you again I don't love you and I still don't want to be married to you?"

Actually, I did want therapy, and I would not have considered it a waste of our time. I thought going to a counselor would help him see what he was doing was not normal behavior for a married man. Even if it didn't help him change his mind, maybe *I* would learn I didn't like him so much. This may have lessened my pain in having to let him go.

His telling me therapy would be a waste of time when we hadn't even fully started the divorce process should have clued me in to his already being over our marriage. Still, I clung to hope, thinking he would change his mind.

"We are just dating – it's not a big deal." (About his affair.)

"You are married, and she is married," I said. "How is that not a big deal?"

During this exchange, he looked at me as if he believed seeing another woman (a married woman, to boot) wasn't a big deal. He told *me* I was overreacting.

"I never said that to you – quit trying to make up things about me." One of his most-used lines.

He often denied entire conversations and I now understood why people often turned to wires, recorders or voice recording apps on their cell phones during divorces. I wish I had done something similar on more than one occasion. Even he might have been surprised by some of the stuff he later tried to deny. Or maybe not. He'd probably just tell me I was overreacting again.

"You need to stop listening to other people and let us take care of our own divorce."

At first, I felt like he really cared about helping me get through our divorce. After all, he always used words like "us" and "ours." Didn't that mean he was still looking after me? As we moved farther along in the process, I realized this was his way of controlling the situation and making sure no one else's opinions outweighed his.

"This would be an easy process if you would just let me handle it."

I would later learn in therapy that this was the narcissist in him coming through. He needed to be in control. However, letting him handle things meant I would lose the possibility of a stable future.

Normally, I had a snappy comeback when pushed into a corner. I wish I had been better prepared to respond to his hurtful statements. Since I inherited my mom's Irish temper, I also was pretty good at 'getting my Irish up.' But when it came to S. and our divorce, it was not a normal situation. I was often left speechless. I don't know if it was shock or intimidation, but I had a difficult time responding to him during conversations.

This was why I wanted so desperately to go to counseling. Not only would S. be able to explain his displeasure with me, but I believed I would be able to tell him how I felt instead of always letting him determine when the conversation was over.

Sometimes I could only find my voice by using text messages. Not always the smartest thing to do, as the written word was two things:

- Easier for me to articulate when I felt I was not actively engaged with the person receiving the text, and

- Permanent.

I kept every text S. and I sent during our divorce...*every single one*. Rereading them, I realized I did say some things to S. via text that I never would have DARED say to his face. I told him I thought he was on drugs or he had an early onset of dementia because he couldn't seem to keep his facts straight. I would never have said those things to him had he been standing right in front of me. Maybe I shouldn't have said them on text either, but I had moments where my emotions got the better of me. You might, too. Be careful! Never put anything into writing or in any form of permanent communication you don't want him to share with his attorney.

And one more thing, texting is also instant. Take a breath and reread your texts before you hit send. Emotional exchanges may allow you to vent some pent-up anger or hurt, but take a step back and make sure the content of your text is truly necessary for him to know before you send it.

**TRUTH**: Things to remember when communicating with your soon-to-be ex:

1. Take what he says with a grain of salt. He's checked out and no longer cares about how you feel. He is only looking out for himself, so you can't believe what he says about the process.

2. Take a 10-minute break and think about things before you respond or react.

3. Protect your heart. S. seemed to know just what to say to hurt me so deeply I would shut down. I had to learn not to let his verbal jabs get to me.

4. Practice your conversations, or at the very least think carefully before you speak. Try not to let emotions get the better of you. Don't say anything that will get you in trouble or lessen his responsibility for what you are going through. Use your support team to vent if needed.

5. Don't let him take you to the dark place he is. That is his space, not yours. I believe S. wanted someone to share in his misery or perhaps somewhere else to lay the blame. I did everything I could to make sure the blame stayed where it needed to be – on him.

## Hard Lesson #4. The man who promised to love and protect you no longer has your best interests in mind.

Once the divorce process starts, it's every person for themselves, literally. I think I avoided coming to terms with this hard fact the most.

In the beginning, I believed S. when he told me he would help me through the divorce process. He had always taken care of things for us before, why wouldn't he do the same now? He told me I could trust him to make sure my future was safe and secure. He told me he wanted to make this process easy on me and not cause me any more pain. He told me he was going to do the right thing for us. *He promised.*

The man who was a problem-solver and a "get your hands dirty" kind of guy now wanted to deny there was anything wrong; ignore it and walk away. He refused to share any of his feelings. He refused to get therapy. It seemed he just wanted out and expected me to be OK with it. Maybe he expected me to hang onto who he used to be and trust he knew what was best for us in our divorce process. He brought this point up repeatedly – that he wanted me to be safe in my future and would do whatever it took to make our divorce easy.

Should I believe the man who was supposed to take care of me as he promised in our wedding vows, and let him handle everything? Or do I believe *every other person on the planet* who was telling me, "Don't trust him!!!"?

S. wanted us to avoid an actual court process by going through mediation. Since I was still convinced he would never do anything to hurt me, I almost agreed to the single lawyer process – even with a chorus of people telling me to get my own lawyer. It wasn't until I discovered my ex-husband was still in contact with the other woman, even though he had told me several times he was not seeing her anymore, I started to think maybe I couldn't trust him to look out for me.

Turned out I was right because once I hired my own lawyer, all bets were off. He went from trying to comfort me and offer advice, to shutting me out and speaking to me only via text, email or through our lawyers.

He let me know I was the irresponsible one for doing research, getting a lawyer of my own and not letting him handle everything through mediation. Yet, when I told him I didn't like the direction his lawyer was taking, he told me he didn't know how the divorce process worked so he was just letting her handle everything. He made no sense anymore. Following his line of reasoning was like following a shadow in a dark hallway. I couldn't see it and had no idea where it was going. I had no choice but to follow, as I had to get to the other side.

**TRUTH**: Those people around you saying your soon-to-be-ex cannot be trusted and you cannot believe what he is telling you--They are right!

**Hard Lesson #5. Not only does he not have your best interests in mind, but he also may do things to hurt you.**

I don't believe anyone gets married so they can get divorced. Entering into marriage, my intent was to be married forever. I guess I never realized forever was so relative.

Since becoming unmarried was not my choice, I had to work through a painful process. For the first several weeks after my husband told me he didn't love me anymore, I fought to keep us together. After he admitted to his affair, I discovered there was something I was not able to forgive him for doing; something I was not willing to work on or fix.

It wasn't even about his being with another woman, but more knowing he was confiding in her about whatever it was he was going through. Was he sharing intimate details of our marriage with her? If so, he was sharing those details *completely unbeknownst to me*. How could he be so hurtful and disrespectful of my feelings?

I believe he knew an affair was a deal-breaker for me, so he went ahead and continued to engage in a relationship with her even though he knew I wanted to reconcile and keep our marriage together. His actions showed he no longer cared me or the relationships with our family and friends. He seemed to only care about himself, and I had to come to terms with that.

As you go through your divorce, you may feel like the man who promised to "love, honor and cherish" you instead seems to loathe, demean and neglect you. What do you do?

The easiest answer is to cut off all ties and communication with him. This may not be very realistic, especially if you have children together. For me, cutting off all ties was nearly impossible to do emotionally. I had been blindsided by his colossal midlife crisis and was still very much in love with him. I believed if he let me help him work through his unhappiness, we could rebuild and be an even stronger couple.

For some women, when they reach the same point in their divorces, emotions akin to hatred have already started to surface. Cutting off contact with their former husband is easier and may actually be a relief.

My letting go was a slow and excruciating process. My friends and family might say I brought it on myself, as they wanted me to just shut him out of my life. I couldn't do it. Even as angry as I was knowing he was lying to me and taking advantage of me, I still couldn't push it all away.

- I knew he had an affair.
- I knew he was trying to convince me to agree to mediation so he could control the financial aspect of the divorce.
- I knew he was just pretending to care about my future.

Yet I kept thinking he was still the man I loved and could trust. I didn't want to believe he meant to completely erase the last twenty-three years so he could start over as if I had never existed. I think I relented to the divorce out of sheer exhaustion. I was trying to convince him our marriage was worth saving, only to discover he wanted to live a different life--without me.

**TRUTH**: Your soon-to-be-ex is only looking out for himself. If you still believe otherwise, please reread this chapter!

**Hard Lesson #6. You cannot believe any of the words that fall out of his mouth.**

My therapist once told me, "Once someone has figured out it is easier to lie than it is to face the questions or conflicts that come from telling the truth, they rarely tell the truth again."

After S. moved out of the house and our in-person communication was limited to when he would come over to help with the lawn or our run-ins at work, there were times when I would hear him talking and not understand a word he was saying. The guy I used to be so in-tune with that I could finish his sentences, was now speaking a language foreign to me. In short, I was amazed by some of the words that fell out of his mouth.

I wasn't sure what hurt me more, the fact that he didn't love me anymore, or that he thought I was so insipid and stupid he could take advantage of me during the divorce process by talking in circles or telling flat out lies. Was he hoping I was too distraught to notice?

In discussing this with some of my fellow divorcees, I found many of these statements were universal. There is simply no Rosetta Stone® program to help you translate what your former spouse is really saying to you.

Here are some examples of the s--t that fell out of my ex's mouth, and my best attempt at translating the true meaning behind those words looking through the lens of an impending   divorce.

**I have to run some errands today, but you don't need to go.**

I am meeting my girlfriend, but I will stop by the store and pick up some yard waste bags and fertilizer to make my errand look legit.

**I plan to spend the evening at the lodge/boat club/bar/fill-in-the-location with the guys for a couple of beers.**

I am meeting my girlfriend, but you trust me unequivocally, so that makes everything A-OK.

**Just because I am friends with her (girlfriend) on Facebook, doesn't mean anything is going on.**

I can plan and scheme with her using Facebook Messenger and it all appears so very innocent.

**I just don't love you anymore.**

I found someone else, and don't want YOU anymore.

**Our marriage was going bad long before I found someone else.**

I'm not going to own any of this. I'll blame you instead.

**I'm saving you from an unhappy future. You don't really want to spend the rest of your life with someone like me.**

The fact I am totally destroying your life can be justified by my turning the story around and making it look like by leaving you, I am doing you a favor.

**Maybe I need to be alone in order to find out what I really need out of life.**

I just want you out of my life quickly, so I can make room for someone else.

**I won't make you leave the house until you find a safe, suitable living arrangement. And I would never charge you rent to live there.**

Even though all the bills are being covered out of our joint funds, I am going to have my lawyer send your lawyer a letter telling you to vacate the premises unless you pay all the bills out of your own pocket. I'm tired of living in my parents' basement.

**No, you take the cats. I wouldn't want to separate them from you.**
I don't want any responsibilities or anything to remind me of our life together.

**You don't need to read the whole document before you sign it – it's just basic legal stuff.**
I don't want you to read the document; because if you do, you will discover you are signing everything over to me.

**My lawyer told me I had to.**
In the quest to *find myself*, I have inadvertently misplaced my balls.

**TRUTH**: Unbelievable. That is what he had become, and don't forget it.

**Hard Lesson #7. You cannot "just get this over with."**

Divorce is HARD. It's emotionally, financially and physically draining. In order to ease some of the pain, you might be tempted to make hasty decisions to avoid having to go to court again, or so you don't have to deal with the process any further. You must resist this temptation. Divorce is final. Let me repeat—Divorce is FINAL. You do not get a do-over, and once the papers are signed, you cannot say, "Hey, wait a minute, I think our marital residence is worth more. Maybe I should have gotten that appraisal before I agreed to the payout."

Take your time and hire all the necessary resources to make sure you are getting what you are entitled to and everything is properly documented.

While doing this, you may need to make some decisions that don't make you feel good. For me, it was the decision of whether or not I wanted to pursue actual physical evidence of his affair. Part of me wanted to gather all the information I could about his affair and how much of *our money* had been spent on her. But another part of me didn't really want the truth, so I talked to a friend who was a private investigator. He reviewed the evidence I had compiled against S. and told me I had enough to convince the court of an affair. S. hadn't done a very good job of hiding what he was up to, which made it pretty easy for me to gather information. The PI was very honest in telling me he could follow S. around to get photographic evidence of where he was spending his time and who he was with.

"I can follow him, find out what he is doing and take pictures of the two of them together, if that's what you want me to do," he said. "But you need to think hard about this. Do you really want to see those pictures?"

I didn't want to see those pictures. Not at all. So, I let it go.

**TRUTH**: You may be tempted to rush things or go all tabloid paparazzi on him to get the sordid details, but stick to the facts and don't get waylaid by the emotional part of what you are going through.

**Hard Lesson #8. Divorce is an adversarial process, which means there will be one winner and one loser.**

You need to decide which one you want to be. I had to come to terms with the fact I had married an extremely competitive man. He was infatuated with bodybuilding, and dedicated to physical fitness. He was involved in sports of some kind his whole life. Football, hockey—any game was a competition for him. And he had to win—always. I knew our divorce process would be no different, but I didn't know he would do things I wouldn't have believed he was capable of— just to save his own behind.

For instance - when it came to our finances, he suddenly had no recollection of how much money we had in our various savings and investment accounts. This from the man who used to brag he could rattle off *to the penny* how much money we had at any given time; and given his knowledge of stock market trends, could even predict where we would be financially over the next several weeks or months. During our divorce, it seemed he couldn't give his own lawyer an accurate account of our finances - not even when it was required by the court.

I think he did this to try and wear me down. Maybe he thought by forcing me to learn finances, something I had no clue about, he could make me give up on the money, thereby leaving more for him. He learned quickly this was not going to happen. Once my legal team and I started digging and seeing the very large differences between what my ex-husband was claiming we had and the actual reported balances from our financial institutions, we left no stone unturned. He may have thought he could beat me in this game of divorce, but he was quite mistaken. Even though I was hurting by what he did, I learned to be like most athletes... and play through the pain.

**TRUTH**: No matter how many times you feel like throwing in the towel, dig in and fight - this is not a game you can afford to lose!

### Hard Lesson #9. Actually, it is all about the money.

Twenty-three years of marriage, and when it all was said and done, it came down to a lousy Excel spreadsheet showing who got what. Ouch.

**TRUTH**: See above. That pretty much covers it.

### Hard Lesson #10. Relationships with family and friends will never be the same again.

People will choose sides, and more than likely you won't get the opportunity to tell your side of the story to friends and family you met through your marriage. This would be called collateral damage. In other words, some relationships end because there would be too much of an investment on your part to try to keep them going - an investment detrimental to your being able to heal and move forward.

Many of the relationships I had with his family faded. For the first several months to a couple of years, I tried very hard to keep in touch. I remained in contact via social media, sent cards and letters, and sent text messages. I tried to maintain relationships with them. It took a while for me to step back and realize I was the one trying to maintain contact. Only one of his siblings and a couple of our nieces and nephews, as well as his mom, ever tried to keep any contact going. The rest might answer an occasional text or social media message, but not much more.

After a couple of years had passed and I noticed I did not get an invitation to the wedding of one of my nieces, I decided enough was enough. If I was the only one trying, and all my contact with them was one-sided, maybe it was time to let those relationships go.

**TRUTH**: Once the dust settles, you may become friendly or at least civil with some of the people you were close to before the divorce, but it will be very different. If you find you are the one constantly reaching out, you may need to reevaluate those relationships. It's OK - rely on your support network. You'll discover the people who stay with you throughout the divorce process and after are the ones truly meant to be in your life.

## Hard Lesson #11. You're on your own, kid.

No matter how great your support system or your team of professionals, the ultimate and final decisions are still up to you. You must choose what is best for your future. Granted, you need the advice of others; including the professionals, but you also need to feel comfortable with your decisions and take your time to thoroughly think things through.

**TRUTH**: You will look back and say, "Geez, I really wish I would have done this or that." But, if you have been careful all along, those things you wish you would have done will be minimal or fairly trivial. Like I really wish I would have taken all The Clash CDs when I left, which I didn't. I guess I'll have to download them from iTunes.

# Chapter Four
## Taking Care of Yourself

### Get Thee to a Therapist!

Before going through my divorce, I didn't think much of therapy. One, I didn't need it and two; I thought it was for people with serious life problems. I thought seeking paid advice to deal with your emotions was for people who couldn't hack it or were unwilling to listen to everyone around them who might be trying to help. I was wrong. Starting therapy was the second-best thing I did during my divorce; after finding a good lawyer, of course.

Realizing I needed therapy was not an easy decision to make. I discovered there was a fine line between being okay and wanting to hurt myself. Maybe it wasn't even a line, more like a ravine. You think you're navigating a pretty sturdy bridge across the gaping ravine, when all of the sudden it becomes a spindly rope bridge and starts to give way. I realized I needed help just as my knees started to buckle and the rope I was clinging to started to tremble and sway.

My reluctance to ask for help was based on two very influential women in my life—my mom & Katharine

Hepburn. Shortly after I was born, my parents and I moved from California, where my mom's family was located, to Michigan, where my dad was from. My mom left her support network nearly 2,000 miles away, deciding to move to Michigan because the job market was better than it was in California. I believe this is why my mom is very no-nonsense when making decisions. Since her family was so far away, she only had her own family to consider when making decisions. Not having her parents and her sister nearby, she believed our family unit was very important. She instilled balance between taking care of her family and taking care of herself into my sister and me. She made sure my sister and I grew up to be independent and compassionate, and prepared us to be ready to handle anything tossed our way. Even though our family unit was extremely tight, we knew when it came right down to it, you need to look out for you.

My other hero is Katharine Hepburn. I love Kate, or at least the idea of her, not ever having been lucky enough to meet her. I have read her memoir, *Me*, so many times I am on my second copy of the book. Years ago, I reluctantly threw away my first copy as I had worn down the binding and the pages were falling out.

I learned a lot from Katharine. She didn't let a lot of people into her inner circle—she was very skeptical—but if you did earn her trust and respect, she was someone you could rely on to be there in even the toughest situations. She admitted her mistakes. And she, like many women, could balance being an independent woman with loving someone so unconditionally she lost herself in the relationship.

For those of you who don't know the story of Katharine Hepburn and Spencer Tracy, she had a decades long love affair with Spencer Tracy, a married man with children. Mr. Tracy and his wife, Louise, led separate lives, though they never divorced. Katharine eventually lived with him for the years leading up to his death. During much of the time they spent together, his wife knew about their affair. In fact, everyone involved supposedly approved this arrangement.

Knowing my own situation, how could a woman who openly engaged in an extramarital affair which lasted decades be someone I admired? I struggled with the contradiction. Maybe I was more drawn to her on-screen persona or her celebrity than the true Katharine. Was Spencer Tracy trying to do right for his family by not divorcing his wife and leaving his children? Was divorce just too taboo back then? I guess it goes back to the biggest question about extramarital affairs. Assuming the parties involved know it is wrong, why go ahead and do it anyway? To me, there was only one answer— selfishness. So, what I mistook as the ability for Katharine to forge her own path may have been nothing more than her wanting everything her way. And since she was a celebrity, it had been easier for me to dismiss her view on relationships than it would be if I knew her in person. Difficult to explain, for sure. And since going through my own divorce, the pedestal I placed her on has fallen a little.

Based on the influence of my mom and Ms. Hepburn, when faced with obstacles or situations I would prefer to avoid, I've always believed I was supposed to *Put on my big girl panties and deal with it! Pull myself up by the bootstraps. Keep a stiff upper lip.* When S. left, I put on my brave face every day, went to work and acted like I was this strong woman who was completely unfazed by it all. I crossed the gaping ravine on the spindly bridge day in, day out. No problem!

In reality, I was falling apart. Co-workers passing in the hallway would ask the usual "How are you?" I would fake a canned response like, "Doing great!" or "I'm fine!" It was a struggle not to turn into a blubbering puddle every time I had to talk to anyone. I tried to pull on my big girl panties every morning. I tried to make it seem like nothing was wrong. But, bit-by-bit I was losing the battle. The bridge was giving way. At any moment, I was going to fall into the ravine. And one day it became very clear I needed help.

Our home was near the lakeshore in West Michigan and in order to get anywhere, I traveled a two-lane road connecting the lakeshore with the main highway heading east. That two-lane road is the only connection, so it gets a lot of traffic. Some of it includes big trucks like freight trucks, farm equipment and tankers. One day, as one of those tanker trucks was barreling toward me, I thought, *All I have to do is move the steering wheel a little bit to the left. If I do it, all this hurt will be over and I won't have to deal with it anymore.* I had to grip the steering wheel of my truck so tight it turned my knuckles white as I fought the urge to turn just a little to the left. That's when I knew I had to get help and fast. I was more vulnerable, more lost than I wanted to admit. The bridge was about to give way.

This couldn't be happening. Why couldn't I be strong and deal with it? This was not what my mom or Katharine would see as acceptable behavior. It was not behavior *I* was going to accept, either. I would not let myself plummet into the ravine.

At work, my boss could tell something was wrong, too. She had been through divorce and saw the signs of the bridge giving way. She gave me the phone number to the therapist who helped her.

A couple weeks passed before I dialed the number. Why was it so difficult to just pick up the phone and make an appointment? Was I admitting I was weak? If seeing a therapist had helped so many people I was close to, why didn't I think it would help me, too? Admitting I needed help was not a sign of weakness. In fact, I discovered when the going gets tough, the tough do get going—and sometimes they go straight to the therapist's office.

In addition to pursuing therapy overall, I needed to decide whether I wanted my therapist to be male or female. Even though the number my boss gave me was for a male therapist, I wasn't sure I wanted to unload all my discontent against my ex-husband on a guy. Would he even understand? Would he tell me it was my fault and if I had been a *better wife*, I wouldn't be in this situation? Maybe I should see a female therapist.

But would doing so be equally as bad? Turning each appointment into a hate-filled-man-bashing session would do nothing to help me move forward. Granted, I might feel better, but even I knew it wouldn't be very constructive. I purposely decided to see a male therapist. Even if I discovered some of the divorce was indeed on me, I didn't want to turn into a hater. I didn't hate all men; I just had a healthy dislike for one of them.

Enter Dr. Help. Fear not, Tami! Making the call to schedule my appointment was actually easy; as was my very first therapy appointment. By the way, they don't give you a little button to wear on your lapel that says *In Therapy*, so no one knows you are seeing a therapist unless you tell them. Guess what? You may find yourself talking about your therapy with others. You might even find yourself quoting your therapist.

It only took two sessions for me to feel completely at ease with Dr. Help, although those first two sessions were a little anxious. *How honest was I supposed to be? What if he asked me questions I didn't want to answer? What if he took his side and told me my ex-husband was right to leave me?* I learned therapy wasn't an interrogation. In fact, Dr. Help didn't really ask me a lot of questions during our sessions. He merely absorbed my telling of the situation, and offered advice on how I should deal with the gamut of emotions that come with ending a long-term marriage. He made sure I felt comfortable talking to him about my relationship with my former husband.

Therapy did require looking at myself for answers. I had to admit I was not perfect. Who knew? In fact, I found out even though I likened myself to being an independent woman, when it came to my marriage and my former husband, I was submissive.

Here I was an independent career woman who did well with business relationships, was outgoing and spoke my mind in social situations, but at home I did what I thought was expected of me as a wife. As *his* wife. I let S. make all the decisions. It's not as though I wasn't capable of speaking my mind, he just made it seem like it would be easier for me if he made the decisions. He chose the restaurants where we ate; he chose the movies or concerts we went to see. He controlled our finances and decided where and when to spend our money. And I went along with everything. Was it his control over me or was it my conservative upbringing? I'm not sure. Outwardly, I never believed being a wife was a duty, but maybe my subconscious saw it differently.

Though S. and I had a great deal in common, there were many hobbies and interests we didn't share. When I wanted to do things I liked—go to the theater to see a play or a musical, I would always have to ask my sister or my besties to go. If he didn't want to do something, we usually didn't do it—even if it was something he knew I would enjoy. I submitted. I was the one to make the sacrifices, but I thought I was supposed to. By letting him make all the decisions, I also believed I was doing what was best for our marriage. In reality, I was letting him keep all the control.

When Dr. Help asked me in my last session what I gained most by coming to therapy, I answered confidently that there were things about me I would not give up to anyone. I would not make sacrifices because it was expected of me. I wouldn't disregard my feelings to make someone else happy. I wouldn't sacrifice everything I wanted for someone else. Not ever again.

"Am I being selfish?" I asked.

"No," he said. "Selfish is doing things for you at the expense of other people's feelings or needs. Deciding not to relent on things you want to do is going to be good for you."

One of the key components to a successful divorce strategy is knowing when you need help. Don't let the bridge start to sway under your feet before you start looking for a professional therapist.

Things to consider when looking for a therapist:

- Get referrals from friends—preferably someone who has gone through a similar divorce as you.

- Find a therapist who works specifically with divorce situations.

- Try out a few and if you aren't comfortable in the first visit, find someone else to help you.

- It helps if your new therapist is a partner with your health insurance provider. Mine was not, but worth every penny!

"Accepting it does not equal liking it." This was something Dr. Help told me on many occasions, and it was one of those key "a-ha" moments in my therapy.

During the beginning of my divorce journey, there were times when I wanted to be like a three-year-old kid who was having a major temper tantrum. I wanted to stomp my feet, pound the chair with my fists and SCREAM. My entire life was being destroyed, and it seemed no one was going to do anything to stop it. Guess what? That was right. No one was going to do anything to stop it, because the only one who could stop it had already accepted it. He checked out and was moving on. I had to accept that. I didn't have to like it, I still don't, but I had to accept it. I am not at total acceptance yet, but I am getting there.

One thing helped me move toward acceptance. It was finally realizing S. didn't deserve me. I had taken a step in the right direction. All through our divorce he tried to tell me he was doing me a favor. I'm getting closer to realizing he was right.

Getting to acceptance is not an easy task and your emotions are going to run the gambit. Dr. Help likened it to the emotions associated with grief. Denial, sadness, loss, anger and other emotions will grip you at different intervals during the process toward acceptance. I'm not going to sugar coat things here. Getting over the end of a twenty-three-year marriage was an emotional roller-coaster. Scratch that. It has been way more intense than a day at the amusement park.

Ever heard of the Vomit Comet? The Vomit Comet is the nickname for a plane used by NASA to give astronauts and other crazy individuals the sensation of weightlessness. It does so by flying in a pattern that pitches the plane up and down in rapid succession to create short intervals of weightlessness. It got its ever-so-descriptive nickname because flying in the plane often brought along a sensation of throwing up. Your emotional ride will be more like that. And that whole throwing up thing? I'll explain more later in this chapter.

One thing I did a lot, and still do, is "undo" the twenty-six years I spent with my former husband. Even though my marriage was unraveling just fine all on its own, I would spend hours agonizing over the tiniest details of what I should have seen or known that could have led to the point where he left. I know (or I hold out hope) that S. did love me at one point. Though he was unhappy toward the end, I hope he was happy some of the time. Since he wouldn't talk to me about any of it, I was left to guess.

During my separation, I would spend my days thinking about signs I should have seen, other opportunities he might have had for affairs and what I did done wrong. My days were filled with *what-if* and *why-didn't-I* thoughts. Not healthy, according to Dr. Help. My focus needed to be on what was ahead of me, not what was in the past.

Should I have paid more attention to my ex-husband's relationships with other women? Probably. Should I have been less tolerant of the time he spent away from me? Sure. Should I have kept a better eye on our finances and where money was being spent? Absolutely. But I trusted him with my whole heart. And I never, ever thought he would lie to me. Yet, he was the one who broke the promises he made to me and smashed the commitments we made to each other. I had to accept what he had done and move on to repair what I could control.

Comparing what you are going through in a divorce to the loss of a loved one is very accurate. I would not dare minimize someone grieving a death, but to me S. was dead. The man I spent my entire adult life being dedicated to and loving unconditionally died. It was that simple. This new version of my ex-husband had killed him. He offered no excuses or reasons for the change; he was just gone. Wiped off the planet, and there was nothing I could do about it. Because S. wouldn't even consider therapy, no matter how much I wanted him to go. Maybe he didn't want to face what he had become. Death by denial, I guess.

# Handling Your Job

Most people who go through divorce don't have the added stress of having to see their soon-to-be-ex at the office five days a week. Unfortunately, that's what happens when your spouse is also a co-worker. Granted, our office was fairly large and, at first, our respective work areas were on separate floors, but running into him at work was a given and happened much more often than I would have liked. Some people can get away with not having to tell their co-workers they are going through hard times outside of work. I was not so lucky there, either. For a while, it felt like EVERYONE in the office knew what was going on in my personal life. I worked very closely with a lot of my colleagues, considering them to be friends, so I didn't mind filling them in on some of the details. Still, going into work every day proved difficult. I had an upset stomach on the ride in every morning, knowing I was going to run into him at some point. I often spent a few minutes sitting in my truck outside the entrance psyching myself up like a professional athlete about to play in a big game. *You can do this, Tami! Don't let him get to you! Only nine hours and you can go home!* Getting into my truck at the end of each workday was its own little victory. I made it through another big one!

At the beginning, when I was still clinging to hope S. and I could reconcile, I tried to protect him. I was careful about who I told, and how much detail I went into, especially after I discovered his affair. Could he get fired over this? I didn't know the answer, and didn't want him to blame me if that actually happened. As time went on, the office rumor mill started spinning, feeding me all sorts of sordid information. At that point, I stopped worrying about his reputation. However, I didn't want him thinking I was the one kicking up dirt in the rumor mill, so I kept quiet at work.

It appeared S. hardly told anyone about our divorce. He may have shared with a few people he considered work friends or a person or two on his team, but not many people knew what was going on between us.

For years, S. and I "owned" teams in a Fantasy Hockey League comprised of several co-workers. I bowed out the season our divorce process started. I made up some excuse about being too busy, and left it at that. Even though I was no longer a part of the league, a couple of people still playing would stop me in the hallways at work and ask if I was keeping up to date on what was happening through my former husband's team.

"Um, no," I said. "He left me in May, so I am not keeping track of anything he does." After an uncomfortable, silent pause, I would pick up the conversation by saying, "I'm going to be OK, though. I'd just rather not hear about what he has going on – especially here at work."

Obviously, S. wasn't telling many of our co-workers he had left me. But then Dr. Help told me the guilty would rather hide.

At work, it came down to this: who should I tell, and how much? A few of my really close co-workers got the whole story. Granted, I had to tell the story in two parts. Part one happened in early May when I told everyone S. wanted a divorce and was leaving me. There was nothing more to share, except he was done with our marriage. He didn't want to try counseling and I was having a very difficult time dealing with the whole thing.

Part Two was shared a few weeks later, when I found out he was leaving me because he was having an affair with a married woman. And that was all I told people at work. No names and not a lot of the details, either. I was embarrassed enough by his behavior, and didn't want any other details floating around the office.

During Part One, I asked those few confidante co-workers not to talk much to others about what I was going through, and they were wonderful because they didn't say a word.

Once Part Two came along, I was fed up. I didn't care who knew. I had gotten to the point where I knew I hadn't done anything wrong and it wasn't me who should be ashamed. My team rallied around me. Even though I had to face him numerous times at work, someone always had my back. I would get warning signals in the hallway if I was headed to the cafeteria and he was there. People were careful not to schedule me in meetings he might attend, or if there were common meetings, I could bow out and get an update later. It was beneficial for me to share my situation with my co-workers, as they helped me get through a situation most people would have hidden from the workplace. Since I really didn't have that option, it was comforting to know my co-workers were looking out for me.

I am normally a very upbeat, friendly person; not a lot of mood-swings, and I consider myself to be well-liked among my peers. During the divorce, I tried to maintain a cheerful outlook, but it took a lot of effort and there were days when the stress of what I was going through put a stranglehold on my sunny disposition. It helped to have co-workers who knew about my situation. They either gave me a wide berth (on those really bad days) or were there with a hug and a "hang in there" when I needed support. Many of them were divorce survivors so they not only sympathized with me; they offered great advice when I asked them how they survived. How did they come to work every day and focus on WORK?!

Here is what helped me deal with the Daily Grind. I'm not sure if these are the best ideas for you. Since I had a job I loved, surrounded by people I enjoyed working with, these were great solutions for me.

I buried myself in my work. I took on extra projects, booked a bunch of meetings to fill up my schedule, worked through lunches and stayed at work until evening. I crammed my schedule so full of work related projects; I didn't have time to concentrate on anything else. From the time I hit my desk in the morning until I turned off my task light and went home, I was *busy*. I'll admit there were days where I wish I had a little time to breathe, but overall, I needed to concentrate wholly on work during office time, so I didn't have to think about being alone in the evenings.

The steady routine was a good solution for me, but at times, to avoid more run-ins with my former husband, I would occasionally get out of the office. Working for a retailer, we were   encouraged to visit the stores in our region to get a feel for how our marketing campaigns looked in our stores and how customers received those campaigns. We spent time visiting competitors in the area to see what they were up to and get ideas to better promote our products. I took advantage of this flexibility and went on store visits so I was able to get out of the office for a few hours each week. It was a break from the office environment, something I needed every now and again.

I stayed busy at work but tried to find balance so I would not get burned out. If I needed a break, I took it. If I needed a day to rest, I took a vacation day. You may struggle at first to find balance, but as you go through the process, you will find what works for you. Just remember, work is a priority. Now more than ever, you need a steady paycheck.

# Health and Wellness

Along with the mental anguish of dealing with my husband leaving; came very real, sometimes scary blows to my physical well-being. I was tossed into turmoil. Between lack of sleep and the struggle to concentrate on anything, I often forgot one important thing--to take care of my physical self. I was so busy trying to bury what was happening to me, I didn't pay any attention to the cues my body was giving me to take better care of myself. All I wanted to do was crawl into a hole and make the world go away. I was constantly fatigued. I stopped working out and I quit eating right. I think I may have even solved the great Diet Debate as I dropped two sizes and nearly 15 pounds in just over two months. No calorie counting, no supplements and I could eat anything I wanted. There was only one caveat—well, actually two. First, I had no appetite, so others forced me to eat; and second, when I started thinking about my situation, it made me puke for what seemed like an hour several times a day.

I called it the Dazed and Dejected Diet, and it's not a diet I would recommend to anyone.

Until my divorce, I considered myself pretty healthy. Being married to S. meant I followed a pretty steady diet plan. No fried foods, not a lot of sweets (unless I could sneak them in); not a lot of unhealthy stuff.

I always tried to eat well and take care of my body. These were an even bigger priority for him, and his *Rules of Proper Diet* were drilled into my head. The Food Police we called him. He was very particular on what food was allowed in the house: nothing fried, little to no red meat, nothing sweet (except what I could smuggle in or hide in my truck), and nothing bad for you or what he deemed as unhealthy. He basically had an approved list of foods that could be eaten in our home. I used to joke with him about it, but looking back, I think he was more serious about food and exercise than I recognized.

One food *event* happened when we were traveling with his parents on one of our Civil War trips. We had just stopped at the Cracker Barrel®, a place his parents loved to eat when traveling. I think Cracker Barrel is the "Golden Arches" for the over sixty crowd? I think older folks can spot a Cracker Barrel from miles away, just like kids spot McDonald's six exits up the highway while on road trips.

Back to dinner at Cracker Barrel. When we were ready to place our order, S. asked for a grilled chicken salad with dressing on the side, of course. When it was his dad's turn to order, he told the waitress he wanted a hot roast beef sandwich with mashed potatoes and gravy.

"Order something else," S. said. "That's not good for you."

I looked at my father-in-law, saw his not-so-happy expression, and tried to make it look like I was concentrating on my menu.

"If you are going to tell me every time I order something, it isn't good for me and I should order something else, you can go sit in the car while we eat our dinner," my father-in-law said. "I can bring your salad out to you."

S. didn't say another word about our food choices. He didn't say much the rest of the meal, for that matter. And taking a cue from my father-in-law, I ordered a hot roast beef sandwich with all the fixings, too. It was delicious!

I have always been Domestically Challenged, which didn't give us any advantages in our overall diet at home, either. I didn't cook much so we ate a lot of cereal, salads, soups and sandwiches – all fairly healthy options. Once we started going through our divorce, I went from not cooking much to not making anything at all. Not even a bowl of cereal. Nothing sounded good to me. Knowing I would probably eat and then go puke (SUCH FUN!) made me to stop eating altogether. This was not normal. I loved food, especially the sweet stuff. During my divorce, you could have offered me the world's largest chocolate cream puff and I would have turned away.

Team Tami saw me starting to waste away, and helped put a stop to it. They would bring me dinner while I was still alone at the house or invite me over for meals, making sure I ate something. I remember many meals with my parents where, like a scene from the Great Hall at Hogwarts from the Harry Potter stories, my plate never seemed to be empty. But it wasn't magic; it was my mom piling more food onto my plate when I wasn't looking. After the meals were finished, everyone would keep me talking and distracted to make sure the food stayed down. Even at work, my co-workers would take turns on "Tami Lunch Duty" to make sure I was eating more than some crackers and a soda.

I discovered eating issues were quite common among women going through a divorce. For some of us, it is rapid weight loss, for others it is weight gain. Many women I spoke to literally could not stop eating. Where watching sports was my escape, theirs was food. They didn't want to prepare meals so they would pick up fast food instead. Or at night, to fight off the boredom and loneliness, they turned to ice cream and potato chips (sometimes together) to fill the void. It is called Emotional Eating, and there are lots of well-documented cases out there. Whatever you encounter, be aware of what is happening to your body and do what you can to minimize the anxiety you feel, as this is normally the root of any eating problems.

As I am well read on the subject, but not a nutritionist by any means, I am sharing a couple of pointers on eating healthfully:

Rule of thumb; follow My Plate from the US Government. Half of your plate should be filled with fruits & veggies, one quarter of it with lean protein and the other quarter with good carbs (whole grains, etc.). Eat the proper portions, and limit snacking to a couple times a day. If you follow those guidelines, you should be eating healthfully. But remember – it is OK to have the things you love, too! Like the yummy goodness from my friend, Little Debbie®. I love Nutty Bars & Chocolate Pies. I just have to remember to balance it with better food choices the rest of the day – and make sure I don't read the nutrition label on the back of the Little Debbie boxes! Ignorance can be bliss when it comes to sweets.

**Drink lots of water**. Since I wasn't eating, that meant I also wasn't drinking much. I would get these massive headaches because I was dehydrated. Though the professionals don't agree on exactly how much water you need, most would say you should drink about a gallon of water a day – not just any liquids, though, water. So, this would be in addition to your daily coffee, soda or other drinks.

Speaking of drinks – let's talk about some drinks that should be consumed only in moderation.

First – caffeine filled sodas and energy drinks. Damn you, Coca-Cola®! Just prior to my divorce, I had managed to kick my decades-long habit of drinking Diet Coke, LOTS of Diet Coke. Looking back, I think I had been relatively Diet Coke free for about a year and a half. I still drank some caffeinated beverages, mostly black tea. Once the roller coaster of the sleepless nights and long workdays began, I jumped right off the soda-free wagon and into a supersized vat of Diet Coke. Over two years later, I am still trying to get back on the wagon, to no avail. Again I say, damn you Coca-Cola! What is in that stuff, anyway?

Energy Drinks = Bad Sugar High followed by Super Bad Sugar CRASH. Enough said.

Finally, another drink we need to be honest and talk about is alcohol. I'm not going to get on my soapbox and preach about what you should or should not drink, as I have been known to imbibe a little. I love beer, wine and really good vodka. The key here is moderation.

**Vodka as a sleep aid.** I was not sleeping well (surprise, surprise) and late at night when I found myself staring at the ceiling, my mind spinning and spinning; all I wanted was an off switch. *If I could just turn off my brain for a few minutes, maybe I could fall asleep.* Some nights, sleep never came. The farther along in the divorce process I was, the worse the nights (and days) became. I was struggling to keep it together at work. Not only was I trying to concentrate on work and not my legal and personal issues, but I was also trudging along trying to operate on little or no sleep, hoping I wouldn't nod off in a meeting or at my desk.

One night as I lay there making shapes out of the shadow patterns on the ceiling; I got fed up, went downstairs to the liquor cabinet and did something very unusual for me. I took a bottle of vodka down from the top shelf, grabbed a tumbler and poured myself a glass of vodka, straight up. I downed it all at once, poured another glass and downed that one, too, and went back upstairs to bed. Guess what? Within a half hour, I was asleep. Success? Not really. Not only did I not feel well the next day, but my sleep was not at all restful or rejuvenating. I had horrible nightmares and woke up several times feeling disoriented. I can see where people would think drinking could be a solution for falling asleep, and I'll admit to using vodka as a sleep aid during a couple of particularly difficult nights. Though I did not necessarily sleep well, at least I wasn't staring at the ceiling watching the fan go round and round.

I know addiction can be a slippery slope. Though I kid about my addiction to Diet Coke and I was able to tell myself vodka was not the answer to my sleeping problems, others are not so lucky. Several women I talked to when writing this book shared using over the counter and/or prescription strength sleep aids. They all shared the same advice. These are only temporary solutions. Don't cause yourself future grief by becoming addicted to any of these substances. It's not worth it. That therapist you are seeing? He can help with substance abuse, too. If you feel you are using drugs or alcohol to help you cope – especially beyond a temporary solution – talk to someone right away. Don't slide down the slippery slope!

I won't try to sugar-coat it, you have a rough road ahead of you, which means you need a clear head and to keep your wits about you. Something you won't be able to do if you are relying on alcohol or other medications to keep you going.

## Staying Active

There will be days when all you want to do is lie in bed or sit on the couch and pretend the world does not exist. This is OK to do on occasion when you need to recharge, but it should not become a regular occurrence, leading to inactivity and turning into a couch potato. Believe it or not, working out and staying active will help you in so many ways. Regular exercise has been proven to help relieve stress, ward off depression, and help you get a more restful night's sleep. You don't have to turn into Jillian Michaels or become a fitness fanatic. All you have to do is dedicate a half hour or so a few times a week to some sort of physical activity.

Here are some suggestions.

**Walking**: I love to walk. When I walk alone, it is a great way to gather and organize my thoughts. Walking with one of the besties offers the perfect time to vent, share gossip or just listen to a good friend. Walking requires no special equipment, except great shoes and who doesn't love shoes? Nor does it require money, like joining a gym. You can still get a great workout. Just put on your comfy walking shoes, put in your ear buds, play your favorite tunes and go!

**Weight lifting**: I have a home gym and know slamming weights around for a few minutes a day is a great stress reliever. I can throw my weight equipment around as much as I want and not do any real damage. So, if you can join a gym and do a little weight training, go for it. It may help you release some pent-up anger, while making you feel stronger and more in control. If you don't have money to join a gym, you can work out at home. Just find enough space in a spare room to build your own mini-gym. You can do this for very little money. Stop by the sporting goods section of your favorite store and you'll see a variety of home gym items at reasonable prices. Here's what I would suggest you invest in:

- Dumb bells (some fitness folks call them hand weights) – buy a couple of sets, one that is comfortable now, and one that makes you work a little bit when you lift them.
- Resistance Bands – these can help you build strength, too.
- Exercise Ball
- Cardio Step

These are basic equipment suggestions. I'd also suggest investing in a couple of fitness DVDs. If you haven't been to the exercise section of most sporting goods stores lately, you'll notice there are hundreds of different exercise DVDs available. Choose a few and alternate them so you don't get bored. The key here is to keep you motivated and moving!

**Cardio**: If you can afford it, get a cardio machine like a treadmill, stationary bike or elliptical machine. If you can't afford a cardio machine, another great way to get in your cardiovascular exercise and have fun is dancing. I'm not talking about signing up for Arthur Murray dance lessons. I'm talking about getting a little crazy and bopping around the room. Spend a good 15-20 minutes (or more if you want!) with your favorite dance tunes and just MOVE. For me, it was putting on my favorite 80's 'jams' and jumping about like a very clumsy flamingo! Don't try to look fancy, just make sure the blinds are closed and then dance like you mean it! It's great fun! You'll be grinning from ear to ear and panting like a dog when you get done. And for a few minutes, you will have gotten lost in the music, not a care in the world. It's probably something you'll need even more than the actual exercise.

## Music

Use it to keep motivated! I love music—and not just my 80's jams, either. While going through the divorce, I noticed there were waaaaaayyyy too many songs playing on the radio that went on and on about love, sex and relationships. Most of the time flipping on the radio usually led to flipping out about my ex-husband and his affair. To solve this, I used my iTunes account to make up my own playlists. Kind of like the "mix-tapes" when we were teenagers. Putting together all the songs we really loved onto cassette tapes to take in the car or put in our Walkman. Today it's all digital! I created playlists I could workout, walk or dance to, and a special playlist to inspire me when I needed a little motivation.

I called this motivational playlist *Tunes for a New Me* and it went like this:

- Pavement Cracks – Annie Lennox
- Stronger (What Doesn't Kill You) – Kelly Clarkson
- Train in Vain – The Clash
- Beautiful Day – U2
- Roar – Katy Perry
- Sledgehammer – Peter Gabriel (This wasn't so much for the song, but the title – as I sometimes *wished* I'd taken a sledgehammer to my former husband's head)
- I Threw a Brick through the Window – U2 (Again, more for the title of the song, as this was something I wanted to do the house of his *friend)*
- Destination Anywhere – The Commitments (I know it isn't the original version of the song, but this one rocks!)
- I Love It – Icona Pop
- Brick House – The Commodores
- Girl's Just Want to Have Fun – Cyndi Lauper
- Dog Days Are Over – Florence + the Machine
- Tick, Tick, Boom – The Hives (BOOM, is right!)
- Don't Tread on Me – Metallica
- Du Hast – Rammstein (This whole song is in German and I have no idea what any of it means, but it's a good ANGRY tune!)

- Invisible – U2 (Did I mention I am a big U2 fan?)
- Sad but True – Metallica
- Monkey Wrench – Foo Fighters
- Don't Stop Me Now – Queen
- Here Comes the Sun – The Beatles
- And no "anti-love" playlist would be complete without... Love Stinks – The J. Giles Band

My playlist was long enough to get me to work and back, and everywhere in between! It also was good to walk to – some of the "angry tunes" helped me ramp up the pace.

**Stress Relief**

Stress is defined by Merriam-Webster as, "a state of mental tension and worry caused by problems in your life, such as work, money, relationships," etc. It is further defined as something that causes strong feelings of worry or anxiety. Both of these definitions were pretty much spot on with how I felt going through my divorce. Before S. left me, I operated on a pretty even keel, able to handle what life tossed at me with agility and grace. After he left, not so much. My stability was overturned and I felt lost at what I should do next. There was a big empty space in front of me and I had to figure out a way to maneuver through it on my own. This caused me a lot of mental tension, as Merriam-Webster put it.

And all this mental tension, or stress, did start to affect my health. If left to think about my predicament too much, I would get chest pains. I became very well acquainted with the blood pressure machine in the lobby of my workplace, as I always felt like my blood pressure was high (it was) and my heart was racing (that, too). It seemed I had overcome wanting to end my own life, only to die of a stress-induced heart attack as I went through my divorce. Great. Is that what Poetic Justice means?

I began to research ways in which I could relieve stress. I hit the bookstore and the library to see what the experts recommended. Wow – we humans sure have a lot of stress! There were shelves and shelves of books giving advice and techniques for relieving stress. Typing stress relief into the search in iBooks or Google brought results of hundreds of books and website suggestions. Some stress relief techniques were obvious; like meditation and overall wellbeing, and some were downright mean; like kissing and sex—gee, thanks. I read through a lot of the suggested books & websites and included some of my favorites in the appendix at the end of this book.

What worked for me? Overall wellness. I found taking care of myself by getting plenty of sleep, eating right and keeping up on my exercise plan helped me reduce stress. However, during a divorce, taking care of you isn't always your first priority. Here are some shortcuts to stress relief to help keep you on track.

**Deep Breathing**: I know it sounds hokey as we all breathe, right? But deep breathing is different than regular breathing. Taking a few deep breaths during stressful moments made me feel calm. Getting the exact breathing techniques down took take a little practice. I learned I was what the experts called a *shallow breather,* which meant I took lots of short, shallow breaths. I had to correct this by making sure when I took a deep breath I used not only my lungs, but also my *thoracic diaphragm,* a fancy definition for the muscle that controls your lung function. When I first started my deep breathing exercises, there were a couple of times I got a little dizzy and felt like I was going to pass out due to lack of oxygen. Kind of like when I was a kid blowing up a whole bunch of balloons. After a few tries, I got the hang of it, making the exercises easier.

Soon, I was using this technique multiple times a day to calm me down. What's great about deep breathing is it can be done often without a lot of people knowing what you are doing, which is way better than breaking things and throwing stuff around to relieve stress.

When you start to feel stress closing in around you, practice deep breathing. Here is how it works. Inhale deeply through your nose making sure to fill your lungs completely using your *thoracic diaphragm.* Hold your breath for a few seconds and then exhale through your mouth, making an audible 'whoosh' sound as you push all the air out. Do this several times, and you should start to feel more relaxed.

**Meditation**: Once I mastered the art of deep breathing I decided to take those calming techniques to the next level. I tried meditation. Even though I read several articles on meditation and had converted part of my gym space into a meditation zone, I soon discovered I might have to enlist the help of the professionals on this one.

My favorite Disney character is Tigger. He is famous for bouncing around a lot. I bounce around even more. Trying to meditate on my own was not working. Even with my eyes closed, and Zen sounds playing on my iPhone app in the background, I was too easily distracted.

To learn proper techniques for meditation and do so in a controlled environment, I enlisted the help of my besties and we signed up for a trial class of yoga. Even though we went into this experiment with the best intentions, we found out two things: Clumsy people should not take yoga. Nor is it suitable for a group of besties prone to giggle fits. We tried to behave, but judging from the looks we received from other class participants and our venerable yogi, yoga wasn't our thing. Even though we took things seriously during the class, we were not asked to come back to try other classes once our trial session ended. Namaste.

Next I tried Tai Chi. Remembering the yoga session; I bought a couple of Tai Chi DVDs to try on my own--at home. According to the DVD boxes, the Tai Chi lessons I bought were supposed to improve balance, concentration and mobility. Honestly, I think I was supposed to have some of those traits to begin with. Though it went better than yoga – Tai Chi also wasn't for the clumsy, or the bouncy. But at least the giggling didn't bother anyone, not even the cats.

I still hope to find someone to teach me actual meditation. I use the deep breathing exercises and Tai Chi for now, but I do think I need to learn actual meditation to help me relax. Seems funny to pay someone to teach me to be still and quiet, but obviously, I'm not very good at it on my own.

**Laugh a Little**: The best stress buster? Laughter.

I've always had a great sense of humor and I don't take myself too seriously. When the divorce started, I lost my shiny, happy personality. After a few sessions of therapy, though, I made a concerted effort to put humor into the situation. Was my life unraveling? Sure it was, but there wasn't anything I could do about it, so why not try to find some humor in it. My journal entries went from 'woe is me' in nature to 'woe is *he*' in nature. I couldn't make him change, but I could make fun of him.

You may need help in keeping your humor. Let your besties help you by either going to see comedies at the movies, or spending a night reminiscing about the silly things you did 'back in the day.' You'll be surprised at how much there is to make you laugh. Laughter really is the best medicine – and you are allowed to get addicted to that drug.

**Doing Things for Yourself:** I was so used to being with S. every day and doing things with him or for him, I felt lost after he left. I realized without his direction, I didn't know what I should be doing. Or more importantly, what I *could* be doing. Our social calendar was usually set by him or involved people from his side of the marriage. After he left, I found myself with a lot of time I didn't quite know how to fill. My besties kept reminding me I didn't have to ask for permission to do anything anymore. I was no longer accountable to him; therefore, I could do things I didn't do while I was living with him. I could do things for me, things that made me happy. Though this is may be an alien concept at first – embrace it! Doing things to make *you* happy is the best side-effect of divorce.

One of the first things I did was to buy myself fresh flowers to put on my nightstand. I love flowers, but my ex-husband had me convinced buying fresh flowers was a waste of money. He would say, "Why spend money on something that will just die in a couple of days anyway?" Reasonable thinking, I guess. While I was married, I never had any fresh flowers around the house unless I picked them from my garden. After he left, I decided buying fresh flowers wasn't a waste of money. They made me feel special during a time when I felt overwhelmed and rejected. Every couple of weeks, I would buy a big bouquet of flowers to put next to the bed. They smelled great and it was nice to have something colorful and pretty to look at first thing in the morning. They cheered me up during a very tumultuous time.

What makes you happy? Don't be afraid to spend a little money on something to cheer you up. Send yourself cards or postcards so you are getting nice stuff in the mail and not just legal notices or bills. Or if you know someone going through a divorce, maybe bring her some flowers, too.

I even got a little crazy and introduced a Sweets Only Saturday. As I mentioned before, sweets were considered contraband in my married household. During the divorce, there were a couple of Saturdays where I was alone and I ate nothing but sweets. Donuts, cookies, ice cream; even candy bars. Only sweet stuff was allowed each meal of the day. I enjoyed shopping for Sweets Only Saturday, too. The grocery shopping trip was much more enjoyable when I was buying stuff previously on the *banned list*! It was exhilarating to be able to carry all those sweets right into the house, as I had gotten used to keeping sweets in my desk at work or hidden in my truck. Sweets Only Saturday ran its course pretty quickly, though, as too many sugar crashes made me realize having an entire day where I didn't eat anything of nutritional value was not ideal. At the time, it served its purpose, though, which was to defy the control I let my former husband have over everything we did, right down to the food we ate. One thing I did learn from Sweets Only Saturday? I can buy and eat what I want. I just have to remember to keep it reasonable. Sweets only in moderation.

**Take a trip**. Did you see the movie, *How Stella Got Her Groove Back?* After a particularly rough divorce, Stella takes a tropical getaway and finds a young (and exceptionally HOT!) companion to help her forget her situation. Maybe a tropical getaway is just what you need to overcome your divorce, but please wait until the divorce is final. My ex-husband took a week-long vacation to Florida just prior to our first court date. Plane tickets, car rental, etc. all purchased using *our* money. It certainly didn't feel great to get that credit card bill, let me tell you! Be careful not to spend joint funds during your divorce, as it can cause problems with financial accountability. Take a rejuvenation vacation once the divorce is final and treat yourself to a little celebratory getaway.

My friends would say a little vacation was just what I needed. I didn't take a real vacation after my divorce, but I did get the opportunity to spend time in Marco Island, Florida for work. I spent my free time on the beach with my toes in the sand. It was great, and I didn't think about much except how nice the scenery was – scenery very different than what I was dealing with at home.

**Things that make you smile**. Some things might seem frivolous, like my buying fresh flowers or eating sweets all day, but as long as they make you happy, set out to do things to make you smile – or at least make you feel better. Buy some new shoes. Go get a Mani-Pedi. Think about what makes you happy, maybe even go back to doing some of the things you used to do. Touch base with who you were before you got married. Since I was only 18 when I met my former husband, this wasn't relevant for me. But some of the women I talked to said after their divorces, they had to reconnect with their former self, and start finding the little things that used to make them happy in order to smile again.

Because my husband had an affair, I felt defective as a woman. Even though Dr. Help told me affairs rarely had anything to do with physical appearance, I believed S. wanted to be with someone else because I was no longer attractive to him. *Was I overweight? Was I out of shape? Was I ugly?* I asked these questions every time I looked in the mirror. Even though I had people telling me it couldn't have been any of those things, I still felt flawed.

I had to get past allowing myself to believe I was somehow less of a woman because S. had found someone else. Whatever problems he perceived were going on, they were his perceptions not my reality. So even though I didn't have a lot of disposable income when I was going through my divorce, I set aside a little bit of money for retail therapy. A new outfit, a new haircut, even a manicure or pedicure made me feel better – a little more confident.

# Keeping Yourself Entertained

When your significant other first leaves, you may find yourself with a lot of extra time on your hands. When I was married, most of our entertainment involved my ex-husband's friends and family. When he left, I found myself cut off from the people I relied on for social engagements. My sister and besties tried to make sure I was keeping busy, but much of that involved going out and spending money, which I didn't want to do. I tried to be very frugal during the divorce, to make sure I wasn't spending joint funds on things S. or his attorney would see as frivolous. I don't know why I was worried. He didn't appear to share the same sentiment. According to our bank statements, he spent more money on restaurants and other entertainment than he did at any time while we were married.

I found myself with a lot of free time, and it seemed many of the things I used to enjoy no longer kept me occupied. Either they allowed my mind to wander, which would make me upset; or they reminded me of things S. and I used to do together. Left to my own devices, I tried to come up with ways to keep myself busy.

Luckily, I had the cats. I have three cats, Riku, Bomber and Kaz. They all have very different personalities and are quite entertaining. Whenever I start writing, my three 'assistants' are always nearby, keeping me company.

Our vet told me animals have a way of sensing discord and unrest. My boys helped me overcome being lonely all those nights I came home from work to an empty house. I would dread the few hours between when I arrived home and when I'd crawl into bed and try to sleep. I think my boys knew something was troubling me, so they were always there to cuddle, purr and meow when I needed someone to talk to. Sometimes I was talking to them so much; I could have sworn they started to answer me back!

**Hobbies:** I love to knit. Sometimes I fancy myself a real knitter, even. I am not as skilled as some knitters, but my yarns stash takes up an entire dresser and keeps growing. The great (or not so great) thing about knitting is you can keep yourself busy while still being able to think about other things. Before S. left I could knit and plan the day, or knit and watch some TV, or just knit and let the silence be golden. Once I was alone, however, this dual purpose meant I could knit and think about what I could say to S. to change his mind, or knit and think about ways I could win him back, or just knit and let the loneliness overwhelm me. I had a couple of projects I would start and stop, but it was so hard to concentrate, I had to stop knitting for a while.

Later I discovered I could knit difficult projects where I had to diligently count my stitches to keep focused. I had to pay attention to every stitch, lest my project turn out like something from the Expressionist period. This kept me busy. At the same time, it was annoying, though, as I preferred my knitting to be easy.

**Reading:** Reading was a great way for me to escape my situation, too. The library and bookstores were sanctuaries from the reality of my personal life. I just had to make sure I didn't read solely to educate myself on divorce. I had to take time out from that and read for entertainment, too.

**Watching TV:** Before my divorce, I was not much of a TV watcher. But on those evenings when I was alone, trying to pass the time before I could tuck myself into bed, I discovered TV can provide a pretty good distraction. I just had to be careful about what I watched. Until I was going through my divorce I didn't pay much attention to what was on TV, nor did I have any idea how many TV programs were about lying, cheating, sex and deceit. Once I was thrown into my own version of a twisted reality show, it seemed every program I watched was about someone getting hurt or betrayed. This was not something I needed to see on TV as I was going through enough of the same in real life, thank you.

I did find a few TV shows that allowed me to escape my dilemma for at least a little while.

Major League Baseball – Go Tigers! Watching baseball all summer helped me the most. I could count on three or four games per week in the evenings or during the long weekend days, and each game would last a couple of hours or more. Watching baseball appealed to my strategic side, so I could easily get wrapped up in what the managers were doing with the starting pitcher rotation, who was working in the bullpen, or what our batting line-up would look like as the game progressed. It provided me with a great reprieve from what I was going through. It not only kept my attention, it prevented me from getting overwhelmed with being alone.

The History Channel and various Discovery channels. These were channels that had what I considered to be "neutral" content. I started watching *Ancient Aliens* on Friday nights, and it reinforced what everyone was telling me – I wasn't crazy after all. This was a pretty far-fetched show and the personalities were something else, but it was an excellent diversion!

I got terribly hooked (pun intended) on *River Monsters* on Animal Planet. There were certain days of the week where there would be *River Monsters* marathons starting when I got home from work and continuing until I tore myself away from the TV and went to bed. The series stars Jeremy Wade, a professional freshwater angler, biologist and TV personality. The show documents his adventures around the globe to catch the world's most horrific river monsters, i.e. Big Scary Fish. Each show was pretty much the same formula, Jeremy traveling to some remote location in search of elusive freshwater monsters terrorizing local villages. The show always concluded the same way, with Jeremy hooking the notorious 'monster' after a mighty battle of wills – but not before the added suspense of extra commercial breaks! The formulaic nature of this program was great during a time when everything was in a state of upheaval. I could rely on Jeremy and his quests to have a predictable ending. Oh, and I now have a new appreciation for my parents' pool, which will be the only place I'll be swimming from now on.

My discovery of television watching also uncovered a new appreciation for the program *Snapped* from the Lifetime Network. I can remember watching this program before S. left me and thinking; *What would push women to this extreme, do they really think they are going to get away with murder?* After he left, if I perused the channel line-up and happened upon an episode of *Snapped*, I would pause to watch the drama unfold. I might have even found myself reaching for a paper and pen just in case I needed to take notes. *OK, if she left the murder weapon in the kitchen pantry, which lead to her getting caught; maybe if I didn't leave the murder weapon in plain sight...?* In reality, it never went that far, but I had a new appreciation for the premise of someone being so angry and hurt she lost all concept of reason and thought her only way out was murder.

As summer turned to fall, I had college and professional football to look forward to, as well as my favorite sport: hockey. All of these proved to be good distractions while I was struggling to keep myself from thinking about my ex-husband or having to come to terms with my very uncertain future. I continue to watch sports as a way of escape, and know my new home will definitely have all of the sports packages on cable!

One last thing about TV watching – and I'll be blunt. The Hallmark Channel is your enemy. No offense to Crown Media® or any Hallmark devotees out there. I am sure the Hallmark Channel is very popular and serves a real purpose for a lot of people. It's just not something I wanted to watch while going through my divorce. The shows on this channel pretty much concentrated on a bunch of what I can only describe as far-fetched love stories that made me want to heave something very heavy at my television.

I do have a few girlfriends who watch many of the shows on Hallmark. They say they live for romance vicariously through the characters on those shows. I was far too jaded, I guess. All I saw was a bunch of hooey. And if there was any truth to those shows, I *must have* been living in a loveless marriage because S. certainly didn't act like *any* of those men. My girlfriends told me not to hold the "hooey-ness" against the network, as the Hallmark Channel fills a very real need for producing happy, encouraging love-stories. Maybe one day I can watch the Hallmark Channel and form a more likable opinion. For now, I'll stick to watching hockey.

**Try Something Out of the Ordinary:** Dr. Help told me it might be beneficial to pick up a hobby that was new to me. Trying new things that didn't constantly remind me of S. and our life together was something he encouraged me to do. According to my besties, I took Dr. Help's advice way too far. Let me explain...

## How the WWE® became my
## PDD (Post Divorce Diversion)

As I said earlier, I was having trouble sleeping when I was alone in the house right after S. left. There were some nights when I just could not lie in bed and watch the ceiling fan spin waiting for the alarm to go off, no matter how many times I told myself to just go to sleep. Since I didn't find much success with the whole vodka as a sleep aid thing, I needed to try something else. Some nights, after realizing I was not going to sleep, I would grab my pillow, a blanket and one or more of the cats and go out to the living room. I'd try to get comfortable on the couch or in the recliner and turn on the TV. Even though I didn't like watching TV when I should be sleeping, I knew lying in bed waiting to get up made me more depressed. So, I'd go see what was on TV and hope I could fall asleep on the couch.

On one of those nights, actually at 2:30 in the morning, I found myself watching reruns of the World's Strongest Man competitions. I LOVE the World's Strongest Man shows. I started watching them in the 1990's when Magnus VerMagnusson was the stud who won many of the competitions. He was my favorite Strongman. S. and I even named our first cat Magnus (RIP, little buddy!). In fact, all my cats are named after Strongmen. That night, I started watching the marathon of Strongman competitions and continued watching them until just before 6 a.m., when it was time to take a shower and go to work.

Watching the World's Strongest Man competitions allowed me get so wrapped up in what I was watching I momentarily escaped the stress of my situation. Soon I realized I shouldn't be spending precious sleeping hours lying on the couch watching dudes lift stones and squat cars. With this wisdom, I decided instead of watching reruns at 2:30 in the morning, I would watch them on YouTube in the evenings, since nothing else was keeping my attention.

Then one night, late in the summer, it happened... While flipping through the channels, I found another TV program covering sports entertainment. This show managed to keep my attention and shut out the horrible things I was going through.

Let me take a step back here. I won't say I am embarrassed to be admitting this to you, Dear Reader, but it took some convincing from my editor on whether or not this topic was relevant to my book. I didn't want to put this particular passage out there, but she said it would be important for me to reveal to you that I found myself caught up in a hobby very uncharacteristic of me. I'll call it my PDD—my Post Divorce Diversion.

You'll recall Dr. Help told me sometimes divorcees needed to find hobbies different from anything we had done before. The best way to forget our situations was to find something outside our normal realm to keep our interest. I certainly took his advice. I became addicted to the WWE. Yes, I am talking about *that* WWE, World Wrestling Entertainment. There, I said it! It's officially out there! You can stop giggling now. Wait, maybe I'm the one giggling!

There I was, in my usual spot on the couch, flipping through channels on my way to watching *River Monsters*, when I happened upon one of the WWE programs. It was *Raw* or *Smack Down*, I don't remember which now. I had watched wrestling back-in-the-day when it was the WWF, World Wrestling Federation, and its rival, the WCW, World Championship Wrestling; but back then it was just casual fandom, as some of my friends found it entertaining.

That night, as I sat alone in the house I would be moving out of soon, something clicked and I ended up watching the whole program. Not once during the show did I think about my divorce, my ex-husband, having to leave my home, or my uncertain future. All I did was watch the action in the ring and try to catch the names and stories of the wrestlers. I discovered WWE programs were on two nights a week. And like anyone who is interested in learning more about something they have just discovered; I researched WWE on the internet, found their website, and downloaded their annual report. What? Reviewing an annual report isn't typical? For me it was, and the more I researched the company and watched WWE, the more fascinated I became. It's a real company, with real athletes, but the stories are fiction—and their fans totally buy into them. Some people go a little far with the whole thing. Team Tami would tell you I've gone too far with it, too. But once I started watching, I kept getting more and more into it.

So, what started as a casual thing, quickly turned into something more. I became (and yep, still am) obsessed with the WWE. I followed the storylines, worked my schedule around their TV schedule and even signed up for their streaming online product, the *WWE Network*. For a long time, I kept my WWE fascination very well hidden. *Raw* was on Monday nights, and *Smack Down* was on Friday nights (at the time). I could watch both shows when I was alone at the house to make those nights a little less overwhelming. It wasn't until I moved back home with my parents that things got, well, silly.

At first, I stopped watching *Raw* and *Smack Down* on TV, and would rely on my WWE app or their website for updates. That didn't last long, however.

One night, when I thought I was alone in the living room, I had flipped the channel over to *Smack Down* and was watching a match with one of my favorite wrestlers. I was so caught up with what was going on in the ring, I didn't realize my sister, who had been in the kitchen, had walked into the living room and was watching me watching WWE.

"What on earth are you watching?" she asked.

"Nothing," I said grabbing the remote, "I was just flipping channels."

"Really? I've been standing here for a few minutes and you're still on the same channel. You're watching the WWE."

"I am NOT!" I said in my best big sister voice. "Go back into the kitchen." I changed the channel back over to *Smack Down* so I wouldn't miss the end of the match I was watching.

"I can't believe you are watching this!" She started laughing.

"So what? It keeps me from thinking about S. for a little while. And it's actually kind of fun."

My sister was also familiar with wrestling. She's a big fan of The Rock (Dwayne Johnson) and Kevin Nash (Yeah, Big Daddy!) Of course, in typical little sister fashion, she had to remind me I used to make fun of her pretty much every time she watched or talked about wrestling. Funny how big sister stuff can come back and bite you years later.

She sat down, watched *Smack Down* with me and a new tradition was born. For a while, it was just our little secret. Eventually, the secret leaked out to the rest of my besties and even to my co-workers. I'm still picked on heavily by both parties. Apparently being a fan of the WWE was very unusual behavior for me. I'm not sure why, as I love most sports, and the transition to supporting wrestling was easy. Still, when I talk about things like *heels*, *babyfaces* and *finishing moves* or I mention any of the wrestlers (I mean Superstars) by name; most people get a sudden case of the giggles, me included.

In the spring following my divorce, my besties and I found out the WWE would be visiting our local sports arena. I was forbidden from purchasing tickets as I had just bought the lot that would soon be the location of my very own home. Frivolous expenditures were out of the question, and a WWE show was *beyond* frivolous, according to Team Tami. Imagine my surprise, two days before the show in June, when Team Tami told me they decided I needed an evening out, and we would be doing something *different*. We were going to see the WWE!

Of course, my besties posted status updates on social media while we were at the event with captions like:

"Didn't think I'd ever be here."

"What are we thinking?"

To thank them for the tickets, I bought the beverages at the event, so it didn't take long before we were all having a great time. Looking around the arena, I was surprised to see a LOT of young kids at this event! The professional wrestling I remembered from back-in-the-day was by no means something you would watch with children present. I thought the WWE had just cleaned things up for their TV shows, but apparently they were considered family-friendly now. Who knew? *Must remember to watch my language*, I noted.

So, my besties and I spent the next three hours learning the ropes (pun intended) of watching a live WWE event. The kids (and parents) sitting near us were a wealth of knowledge as they had attended several live events. Over the course of the evening, we laughed for about three hours straight, chose our favorite wrestlers to root for and pretty much lost our voices by the end of the night.

At the time of this writing, I am a couple of weeks out from attending my fourth live WWE event – all under the guise of a girls' night out with my besties. They may not admit it, but secretly I can tell they are looking forward to going, too! Maybe not as much as I am, but I'm pretty sure it will be a fun night!

That is how the WWE became my PDD, providing a great escape when I needed something to keep me from dwelling on the bad things tossed in my path. Team Tami does pick on me heartily about it, but I don't mind. It's all good fun. And watching a bunch of sweaty guys throwing each other around while wearing spandex trunks and not much else? Well, it's certainly not a bad way to pass the time.

# Chapter Five
## What You Learn About Yourself

**You are stronger than you think.**

In the chaos of my divorce, I felt lost and like I had no control. I likened it to gripping the side of a bullet train, using only my fingernails to hang on. Team Tami was there to tell me I was a strong woman and I could get through anything. Yet, there were times when I did not feel very strong.

I wanted the divorce process to stop. I wanted the confusion to stop. I didn't want to enter into the uncertainty of my new future. I told myself over and over again, *I cannot get through this.* As it turned out, I was wrong and Team Tami was right. I was a strong woman, but I didn't make it through the darkest time in my life on my own.

Even though I didn't want to become unmarried, I didn't have a choice. S. was going through with the divorce and there was nothing I could do to stop it. If I could have been like Samantha from the old TV show *Bewitched*, I would have wiggled my nose and things would have been all better. That never happened. Not only was I not very good at wiggling my nose; no matter how hard I wanted the bad things to go away, they stayed on and tormented me.

"The only way to move is forward," my mom kept telling me. Every time she said that I wanted to yell at her. How could she say that? Dropping the fight and letting myself move forward was relenting—giving in; giving up on my marriage. I wasn't sure I could that. It felt like I would be admitting it was OK to get a divorce.

Later, I realized mom was right. (Isn't she always?) Looking back and dwelling on the past wasn't helping. No matter how terrified I was, I needed to venture into the dark and uncertain future. I needed to start moving forward.

There was a Christmas special we all watched as kids called *Santa Claus is Coming to Town,* where one of the characters was the Winter Warlock. After St. Nick broke the spell keeping winter trapped on his mountain, he didn't think he could change his old ways. In fact, he wasn't sure he could even walk steadily again. I won't break into song here, but some of the lyrics they sang as the Winter Warlock learned to walk were, "Put one foot in front of the other and soon you'll be walking across the floor." That described what I had to do. Tiny steps had me moving forward. Preapproval for loans and contacting a realtor all were some of my tiny steps. Being able to walk past S. at work without breaking down or throwing something at him was another.

With each step, I gained a little more confidence about taking the next step. Soon, just like Winter Warlock, I was walking across the floor.

Those steps were not without setbacks, though, and they tested every bit of strength I had.

At first the things that knocked me back a few steps were tied to new discoveries about my former husband. When we were living separately, people wanted to fill me in on all things related to him. Who was staying at the house, where they would see him, who he was with, on and on they'd chatter. Each time I would be in contact with one of these individuals, I found myself faltering in my quest to keep moving forward. I know they were only trying to help, but hearing about everything related to S. when I still thought I should be with him, didn't help. Instead, it had me questioning whether or not I could survive this ordeal.

S. and I spent nearly one full year after he left seeing each other daily at the office. This definitely didn't help me move forward. Even though I tried avoiding him in the office as much as I possible, I did end up running across him too much for my liking.

One encounter occurred in the cafeteria after S. had been living with his parents for a couple months. I was getting a Diet Coke, per my usual morning routine. When I finished filling my soda cup at the fountain machine, I turned around and he was standing right there.

"Hi," he said.

I was too shocked and dumbfounded to respond.

"How are you? Are you doing OK?"

It took me a second, but I mustered my strength. "No, I am not OK, and I have you to thank for that, don't I?"

He rolled his eyes, turned away and went about his business.

A couple of my coworkers had seen the exchange and couldn't believe his callousness. Thanks to our workplace's grapevine, the word of our encounter spread fast and from that day on, he was pretty much shunned at the office. Most of my colleagues were shocked he had the audacity to be so disrespectful. Knowing my ex-husband, I doubted he saw it as disrespectful at all. He may have thought *I* was the one being disrespectful for not seeing how concerned he was, since he was nice enough to ask how I was doing. Now I am rolling *my* eyes.

I did become stronger with each passing day, but sometimes I got a little over-confident. I had so many people telling me how strong I was, their encouragement fed my ego. I started looking for a house of my own even before the divorce was final. When I couldn't find the *perfect house*, I bought a piece of land and started to design my own house to build. I took on extra projects at work to become more visible to my leadership teams so I could work on getting promoted. I started writing this book with hopes of becoming a writer to supplement my income and fulfil my dream of being a published author. I mentored other women who were going through divorces. I did and did and did. My new mantra was *I don't need help from anyone! I can do this on my own!*

Wow, was I wrong! I had so much going on there were days I didn't do anything at all as it was just too much, and I was way too proud to admit I had taken on more than I could handle. It was times like these when I would lean on Team Tami, especially my family.

My book writing was constant, but I found myself wondering if I should publish a book airing my dirty laundry. I doubted my writing abilities. At the office, my work performance started to suffer as I found myself getting overwhelmed with my workload and my inability to concentrate solely on work when I was at the office.

I was stressed out beyond work, too. I didn't realize the financial expense and the time commitment involved in building my own house. It wasn't until I hired someone just to draft the blue prints for the house I realized I wasn't ready to start working on a new home of my own.

To take something off my plate, I decided  instead of trying to trudge forward on the house just to get it done, I would live another year at the old homestead so I could finish my book. I think my parents could see I was getting overwhelmed, so they steered me in the same direction. Taking the year off also allowed me to save more money to put toward the construction loan.

My work support team took me aside one day and asked me what was going on. My marketing campaigns weren't up to par, and it appeared I was just going through the motions day in and day out. They were right. I set up a new system at work to help me keep track of my projects and make sure I started each day with a task list. I then ended each day crossing off everything I had accomplished. I gave status reports to my bosses on a weekly basis. If my workload was getting to be too much, all I had to do was let them know and we figured out how to even things out.

Sometimes I had to admit I needed a little help from my friends. They were there, no questions asked. Lean on me, they said. Lean I did, and it made me stronger.

# The Phase of
# Not-So-Grateful

Though I tried to remain strong and rise above the big mess my former husband had created, I did have moments where I was not as graceful as I would have liked to be. I have broken these moments into phases:

## Phase One – Stand by Your Man

Perhaps you've seen newscasts where some politician, athlete or celebrity gets caught in an affair and goes on to hold a token, apologetic press conference to repent to the public. While he rambles on about family and trust, trying to sound sincere, the camera pans to his stoic wife, standing by her man. I would ask myself, *what is she doing?* She believed he was working, but in reality, he was chasing women while she was trying to run the family home and create a sanctuary for him. Then he repays her with an affair partnered with public humiliation over his bad decisions. She needed to stand up for herself! Just once I would have loved to see one of those women bludgeon her man with a microphone while the cameras were rolling. Then she could stand triumphantly over him knowing she had done what the viewing audience really wanted to see happen to the guy. Yet, it never seemed to happen.

When I was faced with the same situation, albeit much less public, I didn't beat my man about the head and shoulders, either. I had my *stand by my man* moments, too. For the first several weeks after he left the house and I saw him, I would ask him if he had changed his mind and what I needed to do for him to be happy with me. If I hadn't seen him in a while, I would call his cell phone and leave messages begging him to please come home. I told him if he would just give me a chance, I would do whatever it took and give up anything, if he'd only tell me what to do so we could fix this. I would cry into to the phone, nearly screaming, "Why?!", sounding much like Nancy Kerrigan, the figure skater who was attacked by a rival to prevent her from competing. It was pathetic. I was pathetic. Even after I discovered his affair, I still wanted him back.

## Phase Two – Being Pathetic
## Turns into Temper Tantrums

There were weepy late night text messages telling him I loved him enough for the both of us, so he needed to come home and work things out with me. I begged him for an explanation. When those messages got no response, they were followed with an "ANSWER ME!!!" text—in all capital letters! Those texts then turned nastier and nastier after each discovery about his affair, especially the messages where I confronted him about still being in contact with the woman after he promised he would stop *seeing* her. That's when I found out how I phrased things with S. would become very important. You see, I asked him to stop seeing her, which he claims he did. But, I didn't ask him to not have any further contact with her whatsoever, including text messages, telephone calls, social media; or any other contact, physical, virtual or otherwise!

Unfortunately, his affair and the other woman brought out some of my most ungraceful moments. I started referring to her as his Little Cow Pie, a play on Cutie Pie, and the fact she appeared to be the exact opposite of the ideal body type S. had preached for decades. I even sent him messages asking if he was having fun cow-tipping. I made no apologies about it and still don't. Just because I wanted to do the right thing and be graceful, even honorable; didn't mean I had to stop calling it like I saw it.

Not only were there less-than-graceful texts and messages about his affair, but I also sent a few angry text messages when we had to discuss divorce documents. For example, I kept an appointment with a notary public from one of our mortgage companies, where I was to sign documents releasing me from the financial responsibility of one of our mortgages. Everything had gone as planned until she flipped to the last piece of paper for me to sign, which was a Quit Claim Deed. This document would relinquish not only my financial responsibility, but also my rights and ownership of the property. It was a document our legal teams and other mortgage company had told us *not* to sign until the divorce was final. Our next court date was still several weeks away. Still, there was the Quit Claim Deed, stuck at the bottom of the pile.

I refused to sign it and told him so in a text as I was leaving the parking lot where I had been for the appointment. He sent a text back, calling me some nasty names and said it was 'bullsh-t' for me to delay the process. He also said he was only doing what the loan preparer had told him.

The next day I called said loan preparer and asked about those emails. So, the preparer sent a couple of emails from my ex-husband where *he* specifically asked the Quit Claim Deed be prepared and signed during the closing with the notary. When I forwarded those emails over to S., he claimed he didn't recollect any of those emails. I then asked him if he was being treated for early onset dementia or if he had a drug problem, as those would be good excuses for how he suddenly became so forgetful. Not very graceful of me, I know.

## Phase Three—Those Bad Thoughts

Worse than anything I did, were some of the things I *thought* about doing. During one of my therapy sessions, I explained to Dr. Help I was having some very bad thoughts about my former husband. I would never, ever hurt someone, but I was thinking of ways I could wipe him right off the planet. Thoughts I was not very proud to admit I was having.

"Is this normal?" I asked.

"Very normal." Dr. Help said. "And not something you have to feel bad about. You can think anything you want; you just can't act on those feelings. In fact," he went on, "sometimes it's therapeutic to *think about* where you would bury the bodies."

I was relieved! I never imagined I would be able to wish harm to anyone, especially not the man I spent the last twenty-six years supporting and loving; but I was fighting off thoughts of how I could make him disappear. Yes, I thought it would be easier if he had just died. That felt like the most ungraceful thing of all. I kept thinking *if I was alone with him, and no one would ever know...* What had I become? I decided not to let the way I felt affect me any longer, so I buried those thoughts just as if I was indeed burying bodies.

There may be times when you'll do ungraceful things, too. It happens to all of us going through divorce. Just own what you do and say, and know there may be repercussions for your actions. Make sure whatever you do will not harm you in the divorce process or give you any regrets in the future. Thinking is different than doing, so think whatever you want. And remember, orange is not the most flattering color, so avoid being forced to wear it by the State.

# The Curse of Social Media

Just because I didn't act on some of my bad thoughts, doesn't mean I was without my weaker moments, especially where social media was involved.

Social media is defined by Merriam-Webster as, "forms of electronic communication through which users create online communities to share information, ideas, personal messages, and other content forms of electronic communication."

I used social media to keep in touch with a lot of his family and our mutual friends. At first it was a desperate attempt to keep some connection with my former husband. Yes—I'll totally own that. But as time went on, I had to start unfollowing, and even unfriending, some of those contacts. I didn't need to see him with people we used to spend time with. Had I not been adamant about dealing with this divorce gracefully, I may have been tempted to unleash the virtual Hounds of Hell on everyone even remotely associated with him.

In May, almost immediately after S. told me he no longer wanted to be married to me, he renovated his social media page. And by renovate, I mean he went all HGTV DIY on it! He changed his profile picture, deleted all the photo albums containing any pictures of me, and replaced them with pictures he scanned in from his high school and college days. Remember, this guy was crowding 50 at the time. He also changed his relationship status. It no longer said married, even though he would technically still be married to me for another eight months.

The social media term *following* was easily replaced with the term *stalking* when I was going through my divorce. As tough as I thought I was, I could not fight off the temptation to follow S. on social media – at first. As soon as he left me, I scoured his friends list looking for any information about what he was doing or where he was going. I was looking for an answer to the biggest nagging question: Who was he with? I later learned some of his social media connections were more than just 'friends,' which was a lovely reminder of everything I was going through.

I began to loathe my computer. It was old and would take forever for online pages to load. The knots in my stomach got tighter and tighter as I waited for my social media pages to come up. I knew I wasn't going to be happy with anything I saw about S. or his family, but it seemed I couldn't keep myself from looking. I felt compelled to know what he was doing; even though I really didn't want to know. Whatever he was doing was right there on social media for everyone to see, yet I knew the more I'd look, the more I would hurt.

This sharing of information during a divorce may lead to hurt feelings over and over again. Following my former husband on social media made me feel it was easy for him to erase me out of his life. And maybe it was, but I didn't need the constant reminders. Why did

I keep putting myself through it? Why did I even care what he was up to? I couldn't answer those questions.

After I decided enough was enough and I didn't want to see what was going on with his new life, I unfriended my husband on social media. I felt like I was cutting him out. How could something so trivial have such an effect on my psyche? It should have been liberating, yet it was depressing. In the back of my mind, I had to admit I had no connection with S. Then I had to remind myself it was just Facebook and I was being silly.

Even though I didn't want to know what he was doing, I still wanted to keep in touch with his family and keep up-to-date on our nieces and nephews. So, I remained friends with many of them and by keeping in touch, I did get the occasional shared post or picture of *him*. It always seemed to happen just when I thought I was getting to a better place, too.

Social media allows people to share details about how they are feeling while they are still in the moment. Although social media is a great way to keep everyone in the know, it is also a great way to get yourself into a bunch of trouble, if you don't have your filter on BEFORE you hit 'post.' Remember, once it is out there on the worldwide web, chances are it will never be gone.

I had to give a small lecture to my besties about their social media. Since I felt S. didn't want people to know anything was out of the ordinary, he remained social media friends with some of Team Tami. This was not a smart move on his part. Even though I had stopped stalking him on social media, my besties had not. I think they even took notes. Being social media mavens, once I shared the details of his affair (especially the who) with them, they were very quick to find her among his friends list. Some even sent friend requests to her—which she accepted. Wait, what? Yep. That really happened!

My besties could see I was hurting and because I had chosen to deal with this divorce with as much grace as I could gather, they wanted to do everything they could to help lessen my pain. I appreciated the sentiment, but I didn't want anything negative to show up in social media. They decided they wanted to post details of the affair and tag S. and his Little Cow Pie. I told them *no* many times and when it appeared they weren't going to relent; I did what I thought was the right thing. I told my ex-husband about their plans. Remember, I was trying to deal with my situation with grace, and in all honesty, I was still in love with him. So, I sent a text letting him know he needed to go through his friends list and unfriend anyone associated with me. When he asked me why, I told him the girls were planning to expose him and his indiscretions. Instead of thanking me for giving the advanced notice, he had the audacity to tell me if anything pointing to our divorce showed up on social media he wouldn't be afraid to sue for slander. What? I was giving him a heads-up and he threatens legal action? It was one of those moments where I wanted to smack myself on the forehead for trying to take the high road, as he so obviously had a permanent address on the low road.

Anything posted about the affair on his (and her) social media pages would have allowed S. to play the victim. If Team Tami had posted the sordid details, maybe he could have sought legal action. Even though I had legal documents that affirmed the affair, I'm sure he would have tried to make it seem like Team Tami was out to embarrass him. If S. would have just owned what he had done, I don't think my besties or I would have tried to expose him in social media—or any other way.

As I gathered information for this book, the statement often reiterated by women who had gone through their divorce prior to the internet age was, "I am really glad Social Media wasn't around when I was going through my divorce!" It made total sense to me.

TO THE READER—Should you, or your support team, be tempted to do something on social media, remember it is forever and permanent. Keep the computer keys quiet.

# Your Support Team

## Go Team Tami, Go!

I've always had a phenomenal support team with people who were there for me when I had big decisions to make. Team Tami was comprised of my parents, my sister, a brigade of besties (they are too close for me to just call them my girlfriends) and a group of mentors and co-workers I could count on when I needed help.

I didn't realize, however, when faced with real adversity, people I may have helped in the past, people I didn't even remember making an impression on, came out of the woodwork and rushed to my aid. People I saw more as acquaintances were offering advice and support, checking in on me, and making sure I was OK. Even at work, colleagues would offer advice or take me to lunch just to get me out of the office for a while.

My support system was my safety net, and as the process moved forward, it became more like a spider web. Every morning I would wake up and discover my support system had grown overnight. Another frame had been added, and my safety net was bigger than before.

Dr. Help said I would see this happen and he was right. As people learned about my situation, Team Tami expanded. Some of us would kid we needed t-shirts for the team. Bright green shirts that read *Team Tami* across the front to let everyone know I had people backing me up.

Here's why Team Tami was so great:

- Before I moved out of my marital home, my sister and a couple of my besties took turns staying overnight at my house so I wouldn't be alone. My sister was there nearly every weekend.
- When I moved, one of my besties drove through the night in a severe storm to be at my house at the crack of dawn with my other besties, sister and family to help with the move.
- My parents were out at my house every evening for over two weeks helping me pack twenty-three years' worth of memories into boxes, and take them away to be stored at their house.
- One night, when my neighbors saw it was just my dad and me trying to load up furniture and storage boxes onto a trailer, they came over and put in a full evening's worth of work to help us load the trailer. Then they came back the next night to help-and the night after that.
- The trailer was borrowed from my uncle, who also helped during the moving process.

I had no idea so many people cared about me and wanted to help. Team Tami is the reason why I've written this book. It is my attempt at thanking everyone who was there for me, and to repay what they have done by creating a book to help others who find themselves *suddenly single* searching for their own support team.

# Your Former Spouse's Family

There was another team in this little game of divorce...Team S. Even though it took me a long time to realize this, he did indeed need his team. He was entitled to a support network of his own, and his family held up their end of the bargain.

Though it was difficult to come to terms with S. not wanting to be married to me anymore, it was just as difficult to lose his family. It even seemed as though he had no regard for his own family and friends. He was the one who lied and destroyed trust, yet I was the one who got shut out. It didn't seem fair, but it was exactly what happened.

When I first met my ex-husband's family, I noticed they didn't share their emotions with each other, which was a great deal unlike my family. There didn't seem to be much affection either, which was something I wasn't used to. When S. and I started seriously dating, I set out to change things. I would not leave his parents' home without a hug and kiss for each of them, accompanied by an 'I love you.' I also called his parents Mom & Dad. I'd like to think I made a difference in how they interacted with each other while I was a part of their family.

After being a part of the family for nearly twenty-six years (twenty-three of them as his wife), I expected even though we were no longer going to be together, I would at least try to maintain a relationship with his family. It appeared to be one-sided and I could understand the hesitancy since he was their family member. *How should you deal with a son who broke my heart? How do you address the situation at all?* I didn't know the answers to those questions, and perhaps they didn't either.

In trying to take the higher road, at Christmas, as our divorce process was ending, I wrote letters to his parents and each of his siblings thanking them for the last twenty-three years; telling them I couldn't have handpicked a better family to marry into and I was sad I hadn't seen or heard from them in a long time. I included my new contact information and told them they could reach out to me any time. I got a card back from my in-laws, with a 'miss you' salutation, as well as an unsigned card from one of his siblings. That was pretty much it.

I have maintained some contact with his oldest sister, who lived in the house my ex-husband and I bought to rent to her. She is the only other member of his family to be divorced. I have a newfound respect for what she has been through, as she raised my niece and nephew pretty much on her own and never seemed outwardly affected by her husband's leaving. Interesting how she has been the one to maintain contact, when she was basically put through the ringer when she was going through her own divorce.

I have been in touch with a few of my nieces & nephews who are all from his side of the family. I hate knowing they have been put in the middle if this, but as one of them told me, I will always be their aunt. Even though they are all on my ex-husband's side of the family, I felt they were my kids, too. It has been important they don't feel abandoned by me because of the divorce. They have been a source of light in the new dynamic of my relationship with my former family. S. and I did not have children of our own, so from very early on, I wanted to maintain a close relationship with the kids. I love them very much and they have, for the most part, been very tolerant of the text messages and Facebook posts from their Aunt Tami as she tries to not lose contact with them, and keep up to date with their very busy lives.

As time has passed, several of the kids (I call them kids even though they are all young adults) have asked me what really happened. I tried to answer their questions honestly. At first, I did not tell them the *whole* truth. I told them their uncle wasn't happy and he thought the only way fix his unhappiness was by leaving me. I did not mention the affair to them.

Dr. Help chastised me for not telling the whole truth, which he said was protecting my ex-husband. Maybe it wasn't my place to run around and tell people (especially the kids) what he had done, but having me lie by omission for him was even more unproductive and detrimental to my growth. Even so, I didn't divulge the details of his affair or his repeated attempts to misrepresent our estate to the court, unless someone asked me directly. I was worried I would sound like a bitter divorced woman by 'tattling on him.'

I'm not exactly George Washington, but I do not lie to people. The truth always comes out eventually. Perhaps hearing the truth from me was better than having to discover it on their own. Eventually, I started telling them the *whole truth*. I got the impression they knew what was going on and were relieved to hear the truth.

The old relationships with his family are different now as the closeness and familiarity is gone. When we do see it each other, there is indeed an elephant in the room. To be more accurate, the situation more closely resembled a gigantic Wooly Mammoth squished into a very tiny closet. The Wooly Mammoth sits there wondering if any of us are going to talk about him, as he takes up a great deal of space. But that Wooly Mammoth pretty much gets ignored, since it is easier to ignore than to deal with a less than pleasant situation.

The friends S. and I were social with were for the most part from his side of our relationship. I had my besties, but as far as couples we hung out with, those were all his friends before we started dating. I haven't seen or heard from any of them since the divorce was started. Maybe they were told I had turned into a paranoid, crazy person, and they were better off not having me in their lives. For now, I will let those relationships go. S. is entitled to a support network, too, and eventually they will learn the truth. Maybe they already know.

Being a part of these close relationships for over two decades, I learned a lot about my ex-husband's friends and family. In fact, I learned some things a) they don't know I know; and, b) they would rather I not share with others. As we have determined, my ex-husband was not very good at keeping some secrets, so I know all about his inner circle. Are there skeletons in closets? Let's just say it's more like an archeological burial site. There were affairs, abusive relationships and couples staying together only because they felt they had to for their children. There were also addictions, hidden bank accounts and all sorts of mysteries and surprises. You name it, he probably told me about it. It was a stockpile of ammunition to be armed with had I been bent on getting revenge toward his family and friends. I'd be lying if I told you I never thought about using the information as leverage when he was telling people about our *amicable divorce*, but I didn't. The last thing I needed to do was actually become the crazy, paranoid (not to mention bitter) woman my ex-husband wanted everyone to believe I was. I needed to trust in karma and let it go. It hasn't been easy, and there are days when I think karma has way too much patience, but I am managing.

Speaking of keeping secrets, I sometimes felt like a bit of a hypocrite because I knew of (or at least heard about) affairs conducted by friends; and I chose not to share what I knew about the affair with the other party. I am not angry with the individuals who knew about my ex-husband's affair and didn't tell me. Am I hurt? Yes, but I understand why they didn't say anything. It's not an easy place to be. I do place full blame on S. for putting those people in the horrible situation of knowing what he was up to, while I was still blissfully unaware of his behavior. I hope those individuals are just as angry with him as I am.

You may have times when you feel family and friends have abandoned you because of the divorce. This may not be the case. Perhaps they don't know how to start the conversation or want to bring up anything to hurt you. Sometimes it is easier and more comfortable to sit next to the Wooly Mammoth than it is to try to make it go away. Part of healing is understanding if you want to continue relationships with his family and your mutual friends, you may have to do the heavy lifting. You must proceed without prejudice or bitterness. I constantly reminded myself they probably didn't want this to happen either, and even my ex-husband needed a support network.

# The Divorce Club

I can divide my female friends into four groups:

- Single – Never Married
- Single – Divorce Survivor
- Married – Could be Divorced
- Married – Happily

The two smallest groups are Single—Never Married and sadly, Married—Happily. The largest group is Single—Divorce Survivor; and as I have done research on my book, the group of women who are Married—Could be Divorced seems to be prevalent and growing.

When I was married, I considered myself solidly a member of Married—Happily. S. and I could talk about everything, and I felt we could handle anything thrown our way. Had I been one of the Seven Dwarfs, I would have been Happy. Looking back, maybe I was Dopey.

It wasn't until I found out about his affair; I realized I was the one who thought we could talk about anything. Obviously, there were many things S. felt he couldn't share with me. I don't believe the breakdown was all my fault, though. Communication is supposed to be a two-way street, but I couldn't travel that street if it ultimately ended in a dead end.

I find myself looking at those women who claim to be Married—Happily with a bit of a sideways glance. *Are you really happily married?* But, even after everything I've seen, I still want to believe in marriage and happily ever after. I believed I had a happy marriage with my former husband. After all I've been through; I don't want to *not* believe in love.

As I was going through my divorce, a few of my friends moving on up from Married—Could be Divorced to Single—Divorce Survivor. It reinforced my conviction to write this book! I found myself an unwitting resource for helping these women with their transitions. I have become a bit of an expert in a topic not even in my realm of thinking just a few years ago – offering others advice on navigating a divorce. Something I purposely I set out to do after my husband left me. I wanted to make sure something good came out of all the unpleasantness I had to endure.

As I set out on my divorce journey, I discovered Single—Divorce Survivor was the largest segment of my female friends and acquaintances. A lot of the women I knew were divorced, although I never realized how many until I went looking to them for advice with my situation.

Many of them had great advice to follow, including the two suggestions already discussed: (1) hire a good lawyer and, (2) get yourself into therapy right away. Other pieces of advice were not so stellar. Every woman deals with her own divorce in her own way. I would listen to their advice, ponder the circumstances and repercussions, and then tuck those little nuggets of information away for later consideration—or entertaining conversations during GNO (Girls' Night Out).

In the moment, I almost gave some get-even advice a second thought. Almost. Like one woman telling me she'd help send an anonymous postcard to the workplace of this other women's husband to let him know what his wife was doing with her spare time. The postcard would include my ex-husband's work and home contact information. I admit her suggestion had me thinking, but in the end, I knew anonymous never truly stays anonymous, so I didn't take her up on the offer.

Another piece of advice I didn't follow was to have an affair of my own. This suggestion came up with a few of my divorce survivor friends. My first reaction was shock as S. and I had started dating when I was 18 and a virgin. I had never been intimate with anyone but him. To go out and have a casual affair with someone just to get back at S. made no sense to me. When I asked these women what they gained by having an affair, most of them said they did it because it made them feel less helpless. This is the emotion at the core of going through a divorce. Helplessness. Feeling like we have no control. I felt this way often as I didn't initiate the divorce. I had no idea it was coming and felt like my entire world was ripped out from under me, and there was nothing I could do about it. These women felt the same way and said by having their own affair, they were controlling something; initiating something to make them feel powerful. No matter how misguided the decision, it was their own. Each woman with these revenge affairs, admitted to feeling regret later. It had been a knee-jerk reaction to the pain they were experiencing and the consequences for some were devastating.

Advice from people closer to me—mostly my family and friends—was to, as the Eagles put it, *Get Over It*. They were hurting watching me hurting and thought by telling me to get over it I would stop dwelling on the bad and move forward to a better place. Easier said than done. They knew it and I knew it, but they were right. As clichéd as it sounded, I needed to get over it.

Speaking of clichés, they get thrown around a lot when seeking help from others. When very well intentioned folks tried to help by offering encouraging words, it soon turned into a collection of clichés. Here are some of the ones I heard most often, along with what I wished I could have said in response; if I didn't know in my heart everyone was only trying to help! Besides, no one told me I had to embrace the clichés—so I'll let bygones be bygones and trudge onward and forward.

**Time heals all wounds.**
Are you sure? Because right now mine feel like oozing, festering, gaping holes of pain.

**Time marches on.**
Usually trampling your heart, feelings and sanity underfoot as it goes.

**Keep calm and carry on.**
Please define calm.

Tami Jayne

***Everything happens for a reason.***
Really? And that reason is????

***It is what it is.***
And it is shitty.

***Take one step forward and two steps back.***
Um, which way is up?

***Put on your big girl panties and deal with it.***
I'm wearing about seven pair right now.
Not really helping. Got any other ideas?

***Actions speak louder than words.***
Thinking I'm going to go deaf pretty soon.

***Just roll with it.***
OK, but only if I can use one of these…

**What doesn't kill you makes you stronger.**
I must be She-Ra by now.

**There are other fish in the sea.**
What if I drown first?

**It's his loss.**
Really? Then why do *I* feel like such a loser?

**Cheaters never win.**
Depends on what winning looks like.
He didn't have to move back in with his parents for two years, start over by building a new house, and he quickly found a live-in girlfriend!

**Tomorrow's another day.**
To try to get through without falling into a pit of despair!

**Cross that bridge when you get to it.**
Unless of course it ends up being one of the bridges I was told not to burn and it went up in smoke anyway.

# The Bitter Box

As I have indicated, I didn't initiate the divorce and didn't even know my former husband was unhappy until he decided to leave me. He refused to talk about what he was going through or give me any indication as to why he wanted to leave. No matter how many times I tried to make him listen to me, no matter how I begged or pleaded with him to just tell me what the hell was going on, he wouldn't do it. According to him, by leaving me, he was doing me a favor, so I didn't need to know his reasoning. He told me no amount of counseling or intervention from friends and family was going to change his mind. As of this writing, just over three years after he first told me he wanted out, he has offered no answers, or reasons why he wanted the divorce. We have had no contact whatsoever since he quit working for our former employer.

In talking with other women who have gone through similar divorces, also with no answers or closure, I have noticed a common theme. There are residual pain and unresolved emptiness we have been unable to jettison. Some divorced women have these emotions clinging to them many years after a divorce. No matter which way we turn, the unknown follows us and we just can't shake it. For many, the struggle to end the pain leaves us filling the void with another, equally damaging emotion—bitterness.

I vowed I would accept sadness; I would accept anger; I would even accept a little hatred; but I would NOT accept bitterness. This divorce was not my fault and I would not take ownership of the destruction of our marriage. I was going to rise above and move forward. Had I succumbed to bitterness, I might not have been successful in either of those things.

Bitterness can be gripping, crippling and all encompassing. It radiates outward from its victims like a tornado, leaving a swath of rubble in its wake. I know a lot of bitter divorcees. They are not happy women. Bitterness has become a new lens through which they see every aspect of their life. No longer can they take something at face-value. They see ulterior motives or hidden meanings in everything, as if something or someone is out to get them. Though I don't know what caused their bitterness, I can relate to how they got there.

Anger is one emotion I said I would accept. It is still present. Unlike bitterness, anger is laser focused. I am angry, but at one person, not at everyone or every situation. OK, maybe I am angry with more than just ONE person, but not many; and those folks deserve my wrath.

Bitterness is also sneaky and tries to disguise herself as anger. There were many days when I could feel bitterness creeping in. *How could he do this to me? Twenty-three years of marriage. He took me away from a family I loved as much as my own. All my wonderful memories and our traditions involved members of his family. Those will never be a part of my life – they are gone. Did he lie to everyone we knew about what really happened?* I couldn't control my situation, and bitterness piled on every day with no relief in sight. I felt trapped in a dark alley, waiting to get attacked by the next awful moment.

Worst of all, I could feel bitterness catching up to me—a big, monstrous bitch hiding around the corner waiting to run me over. The Bitter Bitch and her BFF, Ms. Cynical.

Now, I've always been cynical (Dare I say even snarky?). Immediately following my divorce, I was downright scornful! Happy people made me want to vomit. I didn't want to hear about someone getting a promotion, having fun on their vacations or (God forbid) being filled with joyful love.

One of my nephews got engaged early on during my divorce. When I saw the news on Facebook, Ms. Cynical stepped in and gave the post some serious side-eye as I read it over and over again. I had to fight the urge to call my nephew and ask him what the hell he thought he was doing. How could anyone even think about getting married, knowing it might end like this?! Uh-oh. What was I thinking? How could I react like that? He was my nephew! I loved him dearly and wanted him to be happy. Why wasn't I elated he was engaged? What was wrong with me? It wasn't me—it was the Bitter Bitch, trying to exert her power.

I would go to dinner with the besties, thinking if I was distracted enough maybe I could hide from the Bitter Bitch. It never failed. During the course of the evening, someone would start talking about their kids, their job and their normal life. That is when I would feel the Bitter Bitch tapping on my shoulder, or hear her laughing in my ear. She would tell me to just go home where I could wallow in my self-pity and resentment alone. Was I morphing into a Bitter Bitch who couldn't even be around people who were enjoying life? This couldn't be me. I would not allow the Bitter Bitch to take over. I had to find a way to overcome these awful, unwanted feelings.

There wasn't any way to hide from the Bitter Bitch and I wasn't going to outrun her, either. The only way I was getting out of this was to face the ugly gal head on. I needed to identify the cause of the bitterness, acknowledge its existence, and make a conscious effort to let it go. Maybe I should have gone all WWE on her, and beat the Bitter Bitch into submission!

I chose the less violent path and started my Bitter Box. Pinterest Pinners would be very proud.

I went to my favorite craft store one Saturday afternoon and bought a very pretty paper box. It was kind of like a recipe box, but more elaborate, with ribbons and colorful decorations. I set that box in my writing room, and whenever I felt the Bitter Bitch lurking behind or reaching toward me, I would stop whatever I was doing, find a strip of paper, write down the emotion or situation making me feel uneasy and put it in my Bitter Box.

Every few days, I would take my Bitter Box out on the back deck and start a fire in a little cast iron pot I bought just for this purpose. Once the fire was burning, I would undo the pretty ribbons and open my Bitter Box. One at a time, I'd unfold each strip of paper I had collected and read what was written on it aloud. After reading the paper's contents, I would say, "I need to let this go. I will not let the Bitter Bitch get me," and toss the paper into the fire. I repeated the process with every single strip of paper in my Bitter Box. When I was finished, I closed the box, put out the fire and went back inside. I felt as though I had done something productive. I had taken back control and banished the Bitter Bitch into the darkest corner of the alley, even if just for a moment.

Native Americans used fire to cleanse the spirit and to remove negativity and darkness from a place or person. I used the Bitter Box and the burning of my bitter emotions the same way. I did not want to carry around negativity that would threaten my well-being or my confidence. I knew hanging onto bitterness would affect my future. I didn't want to be a Bitter Bitch who couldn't be happy when the kids she loved so much were getting married and starting their own families. I wanted to be happy for them. I wanted to support them. I wanted to love them with all my heart. I wouldn't be able to do these things if I was holding onto what their uncle put me through and attaching those feelings to their happiness.

I still have my Bitter Box. It doesn't fill up nearly as fast as it used to, and now some of those papers contain more experiences and emotions than those caused by or directed toward my ex-husband. In fact, most of my current Bitter Box ramblings seem to be trivial things like traffic issues, or my disdain for standing in the checkout lanes at the grocery store.

When reading some of what's been on those little strips of paper out loud, I sometimes catch myself wondering why I get so upset over the little things. Using a Bitter Box is a good way to identify what keeps us from being free from negativity. Once those emotions are identified, we can begin to let them go. Or, at least, we can watch them go up in smoke.

# Chapter Six

## Letting Go

### Dealing with the "Supposed-to-Be" Events

"Will I still be able to go to Christmas Eve?" I asked S. after he told me he was leaving. At that time, I thought, and he led me to believe, this whole divorce thing might just be a phase he was going through. I don't know why, but I honestly believed nothing was going to change. I would still go to all the gatherings for his family, just as I had for the past twenty-three or more years. After all, I believed his family was my family and I would still attend all the birthday celebrations, picnics at the lake, and our other special events. Except now, we wouldn't be going together. We'd just take separate cars or something. What was I thinking? Of course I would not be going to the family gatherings—period. Someone needed to throw a rock at my head.

There were a few weeks where S. and I tried to co-exist in our house between when he told me about the affair and the end of May when he left me at the house. There were two major family events to lend insight into how seeing his family going forward was going to work (or, as I found out, not work).

One instance was on Mother's Day while S. and I were still trying to live together in our home. Every year, S. and I always brought my mother-in-law a nice potted plant for her porch on Mother's Day. After they moved into a condo, we would go over to their house for an afternoon and plant a large section of annual flowers in their front yard. As an avid gardener, this was always my gift to my mother-in-law. I would plant several flats of flowers in the landscaped areas at their condo, as well as planting her favorite flowers, bright pink petunias, in the window boxes out front.

S. had already told his parents about ending our marriage when it came time to plant the flowers at their condo. This would be the first time I would see them after he shared his news. Because I was convinced he would still come to his senses, I was adamant about not changing our plans for Mother's Day. We went to the garden center, picked up the flats of flowers, and headed to his parents' condo. We spent a few hours planting flowers, and I tried to concentrate on the task at hand. S. and his parents acted as if nothing was different. Spending time together and doing something so normal, gave me hope we I could work together to fix whatever was wrong. After all, his parents were still treating me like I was important to them. They talked to me about the plans for my garden at the house, how many plants I would be putting in, and what veggies I wanted to grow. It seemed like nothing was out of the ordinary.

Yet, I got the impression neither of my in-laws wanted to be left alone with me. If mom had to go back into the house to get anything, she took dad or her son with her. Dad was the same way, staying with the group, or heading into the house only when he had his son or my mother-in-law with him. I didn't realize it in the moment, but looking back, maybe they thought I would pummel them with questions. I probably would have. S. wasn't giving me any idea as to what was going on with him, so maybe his parents would have some insight.

The conversations stayed superfluous, not really discussing anything important. We all did quite well with ignoring the Wooly Mammoth. When it came time to pack up the gardening tools and put things away in the garage, I was finally able to catch my mother-in-law alone for a few moments.

"I'm not really sure what's going on, Mom, but I hope I will be able to do this for your Mother's Day gift next year," I said, fighting to hold back tears.

"I hope you can, too, Tami," she said.

"I don't want to lose this family. After twenty-three years, you are like my own family. And this hurts me so much."

"You will always be my daughter," she looked as if she was going to say more, but Dad and S. came into the garage. I was starting to cry and Mom tapped me on the arm as S. walked to the truck, signaling it was time to go.

I have seen my mother-in-law only a couple of times since then, though she and I do exchange messages via social media every so often. It's unfortunate we have gone from being Casino Buddies to sometimes social media messaging, but I guess we are casualties of the situation.

Another occasion was the Family Memorial Day picnic on the Sunday before Memorial Day. His family always got together at the lake to water ski, go boating and hangout for a picnic. Since I continued to believe it was normal for me to keep going to family events, I attended those festivities.

It was anything but festive. S. didn't speak to me once. The rest of the family acted as if nothing was out of sorts. I had a difficult time hiding my emotions. I wanted to stand on a picnic table and yell at them for not telling S. he was making a big mistake. They should be telling him we needed to get counseling. They needed to talk some sense into him and not let this happen. Not only was the Wooly Mammoth in the room, it had donned a bathing suit and was enjoying a day of sunbathing, swimming and riding on the pontoon boat!

I cried the entire ride home from the lake that Sunday. I cried because I couldn't fix this, whatever it was, and I cried because I didn't want to lose S. or his family. I cried because I knew nothing would be the same again. He was leaving me and all the relationships I had through him and our life together would never be the same.

May was my reality check month. Over the next year I would become very familiar with what I call "The

Supposed-to-Bes." Those times when I knew there was something going on with the family or our friends, and I was *supposed to be* there.

Since I had such a hard time accepting these supposed-to-be events were not going to *be* anymore, I spent many of those special days wandering aimlessly around, feeling like I needed to be somewhere very different than where I was. I felt like a ghost who couldn't come to terms with no longer being in the world of the living. I would float from one part of the empty house to another, not able to get comfortable in any room. All I needed was some rattling chains and to kick in the forlorn moaning sounds and I would have made a very convincing, if not pitiful, lost soul.

Just prior to the 4th of July holiday, which would mean another big family event at the lake, I sent a note to my nieces and nephews telling them I was not going to take part in the celebration. Given how things went Memorial Day, I knew I couldn't handle the event emotionally and didn't want to put a damper on their party. It was a difficult note to write. Each letter I typed reinforced the fact that things would never be the same with his family. I had to acknowledge I was the one being left behind.

I spent the 4th of July evening alone on the swing in the backyard of the house I knew I would soon be leaving. I used to call it my Happy Place, but it was not so happy on July 4th. I should have listened to my friends and found something to do to take my mind off things that night, or joined my neighbors in lighting off their jumbo-sized fireworks. Maybe it would have made me feel better to blow up something.

Ten days later, July 14th, was our 23rd wedding anniversary. In years past, as the extended family gathered at the lake on the 4th of July, my mother-in-law used to show an old video of the 4th of July celebration that occurred ten days prior to our wedding day. S. and I could be seen talking about how excited we were as our wedding was less than two weeks away, both of us looking happy and so young. I'm guessing this particular family moment won't ever be shown at the lake party again.

My wedding anniversary was on a Sunday, so I didn't have to take a day off work, which was a good thing. I never would have made it through the day had I been in the office. Knowing my luck, S. would have sent me a Happy Anniversary email or something equally as brainless. Even though I wanted to spend the day alone at my house, my parents didn't think that was a good idea. I spent what would have been my 23rd wedding anniversary with them, trying to be brave. I only lost it a couple of times, which I thought was pretty darn good.

My dad's the only guy in our family, as my mom, sister and I had him duly outnumbered. Whenever things got overly emotional, dad usually disappeared to the garage or his garden. That Sunday was pretty much the same. When I started to get emotional, dad started to get uncomfortable and made a break for his garden. I knew wanted to help me, but he hated to see his little girl cry. A couple of times, I went to the garden with him. I needed a little dirt therapy, too. We both were reminded of my wedding day. He walked me down the aisle as I cried happy tears. On this day, however, he had to watch his little girl hold back tears of despair as her marriage slid down the drain.

The next major holiday was Halloween. I LOVE Halloween! With the passage of time, my perspective on holiday celebrations was getting better. Halloween seemed a little easier and had more of a celebratory tone than the summer gatherings.

I moved out of the marital house and into my parents' house about three weeks before Halloween. S. never liked Halloween, so I was now free to decorate the crap out of the place, which I did. Plus, I could buy as much Halloween candy as I wanted, which I also did; some for the trick-or-treaters and some for ME! There were my three cats, all of whom are black, so Halloween was a big deal for them, too. I was in a pretty good place and Halloween didn't feel nearly like the other Supposed-to-Be events of the past few months.

However, about a month later, came the first of the Big Three Holidays—Thanksgiving (the other two biggies being Christmas Eve and Christmas Day). When I was growing up, Thanksgiving wasn't a big family event for us. My mom is a retired schoolteacher, so it mostly meant a four-day weekend. Many times, our family tradition was to drive over to Pontiac, Michigan to catch a Detroit Lions football game on Thanksgiving Day. When S. and I were dating and he told me we had plans for a family dinner on Thanksgiving, I thought he was kidding.

"Right," I said. "Our Thanksgiving dinner usually consists of a cold hot dog and a warm soda in the nosebleed section at the Silverdome." Now, that's a Thanksgiving Dinner!

Nope. Apparently on Thanksgiving Day his family has a real dinner with everyone gathered around the dinner table - and there is a turkey. What? And if dinnertime runs over, you must wait until everyone is done eating before watching the football game. Celebrating Thanksgiving in a more *traditional* manner was a difficult adjustment at first, but eventually it became my most treasured family tradition. A tradition I was not eager to give it up in the divorce. The first year after S. left, my stomach was tied in knots just thinking about not being with his family on Thanksgiving Day. By the time Thanksgiving rolled around, my parents would have left the state for the winter, so my sister and I would have to find something to keep me busy. The mom of one of my besties, who believes no one should spend holidays alone, swooped in to rescue me. My sister and I would have Thanksgiving dinner with their family gathered around—including the turkey! Dinner was even scheduled so it would be done in plenty of time to watch the Lions game—in its entirety—on TV.

Next up was Christmas Eve which had always been barely organized chaos with my ex-husband's family. When I first came into the family, S. had one niece.

Over the next several years, nine more kids would join her as our nieces and nephews. The range in ages for all of them was about 15 years, so the bulk of them were small children at the same time. Their grandparents (my former-in-laws) made sure Christmas Eve was the BIG ONE for those kids with lots of gifts, lots of food and even a little singing—much to the dismay of the adults in attendance. When there were eight or nine little kids running around, and 10 or more adults chasing those kids, things got loud and just a bit crazy.

Christmas Eve was usually an exhausting event, but I loved every minute of it. Even when S. and I lived for a few years in Indianapolis, IN we never missed a single Christmas Eve. The five-hour drive to get there from Indy, usually in *fine* Midwest winter weather, never stopped us. We were not going to miss a single second of the biggest family event of the year!

To help me get through my first Christmas Eve without my former family, I planned a nice dinner with my sister and besties. The four of us had a great time together, ending the evening watching the quintessential Christmas Classics *White Christmas* and *A Year without Santa Claus*. Even though it was much calmer than the Christmas Eve I had grown accustomed to, it was a wonderful way to spend the evening. It helped me realize even though I felt like my world was ending, I had a great support system and the best besties in the world.

Before life without my husband, part two of our Christmas celebration meant spending Christmas morning with my parents & sister. I loved opening presents on Christmas morning. Since Christmas was such a big deal for me, seeing people open gifts I had chosen or hand-knit for them made me feel wonderful. The irony was S. was usually one who made out like a bandit when it came to gifts. Mom had always wanted a son, so he got spoiled! I'm sure the tool collection I left behind in the garage when I moved out was comprised mostly of Christmas presents from my parents.

My parents contemplated coming back from their winter home to be there for me on my first Christmas without S. I told them I was going to be OK, and their coming home would make me feel worse; like I was a burden. Besides I shared my mom's aversion to snow-flakes, so I was totally OK with them staying south.

My sister and I spent a quiet Christmas Day togeth-er with the cats. We opened our presents to each other and had our mandatory Christmas Morning egg casse-role breakfast. Then we stayed in our PJs well past noon and ate bad snacks the rest the day. It was differ-ent, but still a great day.

Adjust. That's really the only thing I can say about what you need to do with your family traditions and special occasions. Adjust who you spend them with, what you do and how you celebrate. Just remember to celebrate. Things may look bleak now, but once you *adjust*, it will get easier.

Beyond the holiday traditions with my former husband, I would also have to adjust my attitude around attending family events I was invited to by the kids. As I mentioned before, S. and I did not have children of our own, so I considered our nieces and nephews to be my kids, too. I didn't want any of them to feel I had abandoned them because their uncle left me. And I wanted to do everything I could to make sure they knew I still loved them very much. When the kids invited me to see them, I made my best effort to be there, even if it meant things might be uncomfortable for me if S. was there, too.

The first event I was invited to by one of the kids was my nephew's wedding – and it took place several months after the divorce was final.

To say I had butterflies in my stomach leading up to this wedding would be an understatement. It felt more like a prehistoric battle between pterodactyls going on inside me. The apprehension started when I received the invitation to the wedding in the mail. Even so, I RSVP'd right away to let my nephew and his soon-to-be bride know I would be attending and couldn't wait for the big day.

Still, I was nervous; dare I say even a little bit scared. This would be the first time I had seen S. since he left our workplace that past June, and the first time seeing his parents, siblings and some of the kids since the last, ill-fated Memorial Day picnic. I didn't know what to expect or how I would be treated. Most frighteningly, I didn't know who S. was going to bring as his *plus one.*

A few weeks before his wedding, I had an honest conversation with my nephew. He was my IT support person if I had any issues with my trusty laptop. We met for coffee one afternoon so he could fix a track-pad that decided it wanted to rule the world via my laptop. While he worked, we chatted.

"So, when are we going to hear your side of what happened, Aunt Tami? It's been over a year since he left you. When are you going to be able to talk about it?"

This was the first time anyone from that family, had asked me about the divorce.

"Are you sure you really want to know? It's not a very nice story."

He stopped working on the computer and said, "You need to tell me. That's always been a problem with our family. No one ever wants to talk about anything. But I want to know."

So, I told him everything. I didn't leave any of the details out, either. And when I was done telling my side of the story, he looked at me somewhat stunned—not a look I ever wanted to see on one of 'my kids' faces. For a few seconds, I thought maybe I shouldn't have told him. I didn't want him to think I was bitter or trying to get him to take my side and pit him against his uncle. I was not trying to be a bad person here. I didn't want to put any of the kids in the middle of the situation. However, it did feel good to tell the truth, especially to my nephew.

"Does anyone else in the family know?" he asked.

"I think one of your other uncles knew about the affair before I did, but other than that, I'm not sure the family knows the whole truth."

He shook his head and went back to working on the computer. "You're going to be OK, though, Aunt Tami," he said as he reset my track-pad.

"I know, kiddo," I said. "But it's still hard to believe what your uncle has done, even though it's been several months since he left."

I'm not sure if my nephew told any of the family about our conversation, and I told him it was by no means up to him to keep what we talked about a secret. We chatted a little bit about the wedding and I asked if he was nervous. He said not really, and talked about how he was looking forward to starting his new life with his bride-to-be.

After leaving the coffee shop with a well-behaved laptop, I felt the best I had in months. Finally, I had an opportunity to be honest with someone in the family and it was a relief. More importantly, I was happy the weight had been lifted off my shoulders and there was such a thing as true love—as my nephew would discover.

The wedding took place on a Friday night, one town over from my parents' house, so it was less than a five-minute drive to the church. I arrived a little early so I could see the bride and groom before the ceremony started. When I entered the church, I started bumping into members of my ex's clan almost immediately. Everyone seemed happy to see me, and a couple people seemed surprised I was there. One of his cousins asked, "What's new, Tami?"

"Everything," I said. "Absolutely everything."

"I guess it is all new for you, isn't it?" he said with a smile. "But new in a good way."

I ran into the father of the groom, who took me to the staging area to see my nephew. When I saw him, I started to cry a bit as he was such a handsome young man in his tuxedo. I was so excited for him, and seeing him all grown up on his wedding day made me a bit melancholy. I saw his two siblings, his mother, and of course, the bride. Seeing her in her wedding dress with all her bridesmaids around her brought me back to my Big Day. It was the happiest day of my life, and I hoped they were just as happy as I had been. My wedding day was magical. Not even the divorce would be able to taint the memories of my wedding.

After saying hello to the wedding party, it was time to make my way outside to where the ceremony would take place. It was a gorgeous summer evening in West Michigan, so the wedding was going to be on side lawn of the church. As I walked through the double doors leading outside, I stopped to survey the scene. In fact, each time I went around a corner, or stepped into a new part of the church, I searched. I kept thinking I was going to run into S. and he would act like he did whenever I saw him at work, as if nothing had happened. And I was afraid I would see him with his new plus one.

It was an awkward thought, my former husband attending our nephew's wedding with another woman. I'd heard rumors for several weeks he was seeing someone. I didn't want confirmation of those rumors. I tried to hold my head high, though. If I did end up running into him, I didn't want him to see my anxiety.

The setting was beautiful, with white folding chairs set up on the lawn. The angle of the sun gave the whole scene a golden hue. What a perfect place for a wedding ceremony.

With the way the chairs were situated, on a slight downward slope toward the front row, I could see everyone from the back, and noticed there was one person missing from the area where the family was sitting. S. was the only family member not in attendance. Since the wedding was still a few minutes from starting, I sat off to one side in the back, so if he did come in late, he wouldn't walk past me. I was certain he was going to show, not believing he would skip his own nephew's wedding.

As it turned out, I didn't have to worry about seeing him. He didn't attend. To be honest, I was happy. I knew the wedding was going to be an uncomfortable event. I knew I might have to deal with the emotion of seeing him and who he was now dating. Yet I was willing to put everything aside for my nephew. Later I found out he didn't go to the wedding because he didn't want *me* to be uncomfortable. Really? Or could it be he didn't want to sit in a place of worship and listen to a minister tell our nephew and his bride about the seriousness of the institution of marriage? Maybe he didn't want to be reminded of our wedding day as the newlyweds discovered the promises they were making today were not to be taken lightly, and wedding vows are forever – not for as long as you feel like honoring them?

It was not easy for me to hear the minister talk about marriage, either. It hurt to hear him describe what marriage stood for, knowing my former husband not only couldn't keep his end of the bargain, but he didn't seem even remotely interested in giving us a chance. I cried happy tears for my nephew and his lovely bride, yet another part of me was sad. Why didn't S. place as much value on our marriage as I did? How was it so easy for him to break promises and vows that were supposed to be forever?

When the newlyweds were releasing the guests from the beautiful outdoor chapel, and it was my turn to say congratulations and go back inside, I gave them each a big hug.

"Those are some very big promises you made to each other today," I said.

"I know, Aunt Tami," my nephew said, holding his lovely bride's hand in his.

"Keep them," I said, holding back tears.

They both nodded and smiled at each other.

The reception was a wonderful event, even though I had an uneasy feeling my ex-husband might still show up just for the reception. Something I could imagine him doing, even though it was rude only to go for the free food. Luckily, I didn't need to worry. He didn't show up for the reception, either.

All in all, I had a great time at my nephew's wedding. I now had a new niece, and I was so glad for the opportunity to share their celebration. I was able to spend time with S.'s family and, although we didn't go into detail about him or the divorce, I had a feeling maybe his family knew more about what he had done than I thought. His aunt, whom I sat with for dinner, told me I looked wonderful and happy, and there was someone out there who deserved me and would take good care of me. It seemed S. hadn't had a lot of contact with his family as of late. A funny turn of events from someone who always said family was so important to him.

Even his mother told me she hoped one day I could be happy on my own. As I was sitting with her and my former father-in-law after dinner, she told me they both missed me very much and she was sorry for the awkward situation we were now in. When I told her the situation was caused by her son, she put her hand on my arm, and said, "I know."

When the party started to wind down and people began to leave, I said my goodbyes to the family I had missed so much. I promised to keep in touch and send them updates on everything from building my new house to writing my book. I told the happy couple to have fun on their honeymoon and gave them each a hug goodbye.

Later, back at my parents' house, I sat outside on their backyard swing enjoying the rest of the summer night. As the moon shown down through the trees, I reflected on the events of the past few hours. The family didn't ignore me and they didn't ignore the situation. They told me they missed me, and like my former mother-in-law said, it was an awkward situation we now had to navigate. However, it was a situation I, at least, was willing to deal with head on. I wasn't going to shy away from being uncomfortable or anxious at these gatherings. I was going to be there to show my support. Because I still loved his family. No matter what had happened they needed to know how I felt.

I continued to maintain contact with the kids through social media and text messages. I could keep up on school, sports and other things they were doing. During the first winter, my youngest nephew, who was 14 years old, emailed me his hockey schedule. Most of the games I was unable to attend due the location and timing of his games. However, one evening toward the end of his hockey season, I got a message from him telling me his team had made the championship and the games were later in the evenings. He asked if I would be able to watch him play. A hockey championship? I let him know right away I would be there.

Unfortunately, the games would be out on the lakeshore which had begun to represent enemy territory. I was a nervous wreck any time I had to go back there. It was hard enough going back there with friends when I was fairly certain I *wouldn't* run into my ex-husband. It was ten times worse when there was the slightest chance he was going to be in the same place at the same time. I kept telling myself I didn't need to worry about him attending the hockey game. It was on a Monday, and Mondays were always gym nights for my ex-husband. God forbid something interfere with a gym night. For twenty-three years, we planned everything we did around his gym nights. It was a pretty safe bet he wouldn't be at my nephew's game, as he didn't cancel going to the gym, not even for family.

Still, I was nervous. Along with not wanting to run into S., I didn't know how my nephew's parents would react to my being there. Would they avoid being around me? Would I end up sitting alone? Just in case, I took one of my besties with me for moral support.

The game was at LC Walker Arena, which added to my anxiety. The LC, as it was affectionately called, was the place S. took me on our first official date, a Muskegon Lumberjacks hockey game back in late 1987. During our time together, we went to a lot of hockey games at the LC. I even went to watch him play a couple of pick-up hockey games there back in the day. The kids' graduation ceremonies happened there, so the old arena held a lot of fond memories for me. But I knew I had to be there for my nephew. I had received a personal invitation and I was not about to let him down.

My bestie and I showed up a little early. We had time to figure out if my nephew's team was considered the home team or the away team, which would determine the side of the arena where we would sit. As we were asking some of the parents already in their seats which team they were here to see, I found my former sister-in-law and brother-in-law. I hadn't seen them since my other nephew's wedding (this nephew's older brother), which had been several months earlier.

This brother-in-law and I always had a lot in common, so we started a conversation right away. In fact, had someone not familiar with the situation seen us, they might have thought nothing was amiss. Not so much with my sister-in-law. She only had short responses to my direct questions during the game. It was awkward, and gave me the feeling my nephew might not have let them know I was going to be there.

My brother-in-law and I continued to chat about my nephew's team and the game. His team lost, but he played well. I stayed behind after the game so I could see him as he was leaving the locker room. Both my bestie and I tried to make polite conversation with my sister-in-law, but it was uncomfortable.

Luckily, he didn't take long to get out to the waiting area and soon he was walking down the hallway toward us. It had been several months since I saw him at his brother's wedding and he was getting so tall. His voice had changed, too, so when he said hi to me and thanked me for coming to the game he didn't sound like my youngest nephew. He was turning into a young man. It was another reminder I was being left behind when it came to the family. My nephew was growing up and somehow I'd missed it.

Turned out I was right about my sister-in-law not getting advanced warning I would be at her son's game. The morning after the game, I got a text message from her apologizing for not saying much to me. She told me she wasn't expecting me to be there and didn't know how to react. I responded saying it was OK and I understood. I wanted her to know I still loved them all very much, and I hoped things wouldn't have to be uncomfortable when we were around each other.

I didn't hold what my ex-husband did to me against his family. I wished things between us didn't have to be so different and uncomfortable. It's what happens in a divorce. Maybe that's the reason why at a wedding the guests sit on one side of the church or the other—the bride's team on her side and the groom's team on his. This way, if something does go wrong, everyone knows how they're supposed to line up.

# Social Media

## How to unfriend with dignity and purpose.

I've never been a big fan of social media, although I understand it is the way most people communicate nowadays. But for me, it was a reminder of how my former husband kept in touch with other women, so my aversion to social media was well justified. In keeping connected with some of my ex-husband's family and friends through social media, I should have known I would eventually see posts of my ex that would make me upset. The picture of him posted by my in-laws as he celebrated his 50th birthday with one of his lovelies (as the besties call her, dripping with sarcasm) was the kicker. My first reaction was, *How dare they? Didn't they know they were still connected to me and I might see that picture and be hurt by it?* Oh, wait. They were part of his support team, remember? I knew they had all moved on. It was just me who was still stuck in the muddy mess called hurt.

I decided most of his friends and family no longer needed to be a part of my social media network. Seeing his picture sparked me. It was a call to action. He had moved on and I had been replaced. I needed to move on and get my life in order, too.

# Necessary Adjustments

Adjusting to your newly single life will take time. I am three years past when S. first told me he wanted out, and I have learned time does indeed heal (oh no, cliché!). But it is a process, and the amount of actual time needed to heal isn't the same for everyone. Even though you may have impatient people around you telling you to move on, rushing things might make it worse. I have written and rewritten sections of this book several times since I first started. Some of my earlier writings shocked me as they contained a lot of anger, hurt and confusion. Now, three years later, I can look back at my situation through a softer lens. I am still very angry at S., and I think I will be until I can get answers as to why he thought ending our marriage was his only course of action toward happiness.

Throughout our divorce he wanted me to believe he was doing me a favor. Maybe he was right.

Remember when I talked about Dr. Help telling me to try new things and be flexible to change so I could adjust to the overhaul of my post-divorce life? Sometimes I was forced to try new things out of necessity – simply because no one was there to do anything for me anymore. The saying goes marriage is 50/50. During the divorce, I tried to get S. to still take responsibility for some of his 50. I was living in the house by myself, which meant all the household responsibilities fell to me. It pissed me off a bit, so to make sure he still had some of the household chores, I told him he needed to take care of the lawn on the weekends. It just didn't seem right. He was walking away from the marriage and leaving me to take care of everything, while he got to live like a college student in the basement of his parents' condo.

After the divorce and I was on my own, I was forced to take on new, very foreign responsibilities. Like finances, auto repair, grocery shopping and even killing spiders – all by myself. I made a lot of mistakes with these new 'hobbies.' Especially the ones related to learning finances. And killing spiders. Author's note: DO NOT try to kill spiders with a hammer or a lighter. Just don't do it.

# Chapter Seven
## The F-Word and
## Other Practical Advice

I used to think there was only one F-word. You know, the one forbidden by the FCC, yet it gets dropped at nearly every award show on TV. After going through my divorce, however, I discovered there was another one—Finance. I am not a numbers girl—never have been, probably never will be. I didn't like math in school and I still don't like having to work with numbers or measurements of any kind. I even shudder when confronted with my online banking.

Believe it or not, I was the Marketing Manager at a credit union for a couple of years, which meant I helped cover the branch manager duties. I didn't enjoy it—and knowing I was handling other people's money made me even more uncomfortable than trying to keep track of my own. Luckily, I hid my fear of all things financial very well.

I must admit through my entire marriage I did nothing with our finances. The only checks I ever wrote were to my hairdresser. Seriously. I do know I made money, as I was never unemployed while I was married. Wait—I did have one brief period early on in our marriage where, while working for a fashion retailer, I had a near meltdown. I begged S.to let me stop working for a while to concentrate on finding more meaningful employment in the Marketing field. He agreed to this at first, but after having him hound me about not having a job for about six weeks, I reluctantly went back to retail. As I said, I made money—I just never paid attention to what happened once it landed in our bank account. The finances were his responsibility. I cleaned the toilets. He paid the bills. Seemed like a fair trade to me at the time.

Since I went right from living with my parents to living with my new husband who had lived on his own before, I let him make all the financial decisions. I should have been more engaged in our finances from the very start of our marriage. Shame on me for not doing so. Perhaps I would have discovered the truth about him much earlier if I had paid more attention to our money and where it was going. Since I didn't have anything to do with the bookkeeping, it made it very easy for S. to hide things from me and I believe he took full advantage of my financial disconnect during his affair.

This brings me back to my new F-word. During the divorce, I had to give myself a crash course in dealing with bills and finance.

An example of how clueless I was became evident when I was updating my marital status and organizing financial paperwork. Several months after my divorce was final, I was getting pre-approved for loans in case I found a house. I needed to print out the past few paystubs for the loan officer. As I was printing and filing my most recent paystubs, I noticed my tax withholding status was still listed as M for married. *How can that be? I updated my human resources profile in our company intranet weeks ago. They must have missed it.* I called our internal helpline to see if they made an error in updating my profile.

"Hi, this is Tami Rake," I said. "I have been looking through past paystubs and see I am still listed as married. I updated my employee profile in January after my divorce was final and it doesn't look like it got changed in the system. Can you see if it got submitted correctly?"

"Did you update your W-4?" asked the employee relations rep.

"My what?"

"Your W-4," the rep said. "The tax document that changes your status. The online W-4 is also located in your profile."

"You don't update the W-4 for me?" I asked.

"Um, no. You need to fill out the online W-4 so we can submit it to the IRS."

"Oh, OK. Thanks for your help," I said rather meekly before hanging up the phone.

I logged back into my employee profile—sure enough, there was a section for my W-4. By the way, there are two forms to submit, one for the Federal government and one for the State. I missed the second one on the first time around. As it was, it took me three tries over three separate weeks to get it right.

I hope the IRS doesn't come looking for me wondering why I had three different status changes in three weeks. They don't track you down for multiple submittals, do they?

After I had my real, final paystub taken care of, I could see it sure didn't pay to be single—I lost just over $40 a week by claiming Single, One Dependent, which I needed to do, as by claiming a single dependent, I could keep more of my weekly pay. Still, losing $40 a week was a shock and didn't seem fair.

Now I wonder how I could go about getting Social Security numbers for my cats. They *absolutely depend* on me, so why can't I claim them as dependents? Unless claiming three cats as dependents on my W-4 officially makes me The Crazy Cat Lady.

Working out the tax withholding status was just the beginning of my financial follies. Now that I had sole control over all the assets I received in the settlement, I was a little lost as to where to begin. Check that - I was a lot lost. Even now I have very little idea what is going on with my money. I know how much I have and what types of investments are 'in my portfolio' (don't I sound all fiscally savvy?), but other than knowing I have a few shares of Tiffany & Co., I'm not sure what's what. Annuities, 401Ks, IRAs, Roth IRAs...it's all Greek to me. In fact, I think Greek is easier to understand. I can recite every god in the Greek Pantheon, but don't ask me what a variable interest rate is. Luckily, I have a good financial advisor. I tell him my financial goals, and he takes care of the rest. I pretend to pay attention in the meetings I schedule with him, and he pretends not to notice I am not really paying attention. It all works out quite well.

I will say this—no matter how tempting it may be, do not sacrifice your future just to get through the here and now, if possible. Yes, you *can* liquidate IRAs and you *can* borrow against your 401K through your employer. You *can* cash out some mutual funds and other investments. But just because you *can* do a lot of these things, doesn't mean you *should*. Moving money in and out of certain funds and cashing out some of your investments will cost you significantly in taxes and other penalties. Don't sacrifice any of your retirement money—unless you absolutely have to—and a professional can tell you what 'absolutely have to' really means. Of course, if you are in danger of not having a place to live or food for your children, you may need another course of action.

Having shared with you what I learned about finance, in all honesty, when it comes to working through your own finances, my advice is to seek professional help. I was playing catch-up and didn't have time to find answers through the internet or by reading books on finance. You may find yourself having to make quick decisions regarding money during your divorce process too, and you don't want to make guesses or estimates when it comes to your financial stability. So, even though you are responsible for the decisions, hiring a financial advisor or even talking to someone at your bank or credit union should get you started with the basics.

# Financial Tips

What follows are some very basic financial tips and terms, based on my experience as I set up my new household after the divorce.

ROLLING OVER –

'Rolling over' a 401K doesn't get you any cash. I asked my financial advisor why I couldn't just 'roll that money over' into my savings account. Apparently, it doesn't work like that. So, my Roll Over 401K is now just A Different 401K. Glad I went to school for Advertising. Geesh.

PAYING BILLS –

One month goes by REALLY FAST. Bills are normally paid by the month, and I realize now more than ever one month isn't very long. Before I knew it, my damn VISA® bill was due—again. And I've nearly missed it on more than one occasion.

Set up a system so you remember to PAY YOUR BILLS ON TIME! My credit score got dinged enough during the divorce from the various monetary establishments checking my credit and reviewing my financial history, I didn't need to be late on my bills, too.

At first, my system was my sister. She and I had similar bill schedules, so when she paid hers, she made sure I paid mine. Later, since I knew I needed to pay bills on my own, my system was to set up a lot of my bills on autopay. Autopay features are a great way to make sure your bills get paid on time, but be careful! Out of sight really can mean out of mind. If you are paying your bills automatically, you could overdraw your account, or miss something important going on with your balances. Don't put your bills on autopay unless you are sure you will always have enough money in your account to cover those bills.

SAVINGS –

I found the best way to save money was to set aside a small amount directly from my paycheck each week in an account at a separate financial institution and then pretend that money didn't exist. I never activated the debit card to the account, and I locked the checkbook assigned to it in a drawer. It was money I had to hide from myself to make sure I would only use it in an absolute emergency. And cute shoes, though important, would not qualify as an absolute emergency.

Using a debit card instead of carrying cash around helped me spend less money. I could talk myself out of using a debit card for sodas, snacks and other small purchases. Having cash at the ready was too easily spent.

For one of my fellow divorcees, the opposite was true. She carried around the "Dave Ramsey Organizer" as she called it. She took out an allotted amount of cash each week and assigned certain amounts to expenses or bills she could pay in cash. She also had a portion of the cash assigned to 'Me' in her organizer, which was personal spending money. I am certain a large portion of her Me Money went to our GNOs (Girls' Night Out)!

Whatever works for you, it is very important to have extra savings set aside, no matter how small the amount. Like one of those online catchphrases, "The only thing certain in life is uncertainty." You want to have money set aside in case one of those uncertainties rears its ugly head. Again, shoe sales do not qualify.

BUDGETING –

I spend how much each month on the cats?! Once the dust from the divorce had settled a bit, I sat down with a piece of paper and mapped out a budget. Basically, it showed how much I made per month, minus everything I spent each month. The first time I laid this all out, it was a pretty eye-opening experience; and I was saving money by living with my parents. As I prepared to move into my new home, the 'expenses' side of the budget got a little scarier.

# Budget

## % of Income Spent

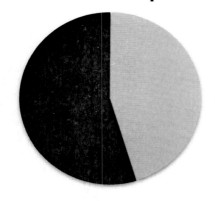

55%

## Summary

Total Monthly Income
$3,750

Total Monthly Expenses
$2,058

Total Monthly Savings
$550

Cash Balance
$1,142

## Monthly Income

| Item | Amount |
| --- | --- |
| Income Source 1 | $2,500.00 |
| Income Source 2 | $1,000.00 |
| Other | $250.00 |

# Monthly Expenses

| Item | Amount |
|---|---|
| Rent/mortgage | $800.00 |
| Electric | $120.00 |
| Gas | $50.00 |
| Cell phone | $45.00 |
| Groceries | $500.00 |
| Car payment | $273.00 |
| Credit cards | $120.00 |
| Auto insurance | $50.00 |
| Miscellaneous | $100.00 |

# Monthly Savings

| Date | Amount |
|---|---|
| [Date] | $200.00 |
| [Date] | $250.00 |
| [Date] | $100.00 |

If you aren't sure where to start, talk to your bank or credit union, or visit their website to look for ways to set up a household budget. You can also do what I did for the example above and pull a template from

Microsoft Excel – enter your income, expenses and estimated savings and  ba-da-bing – It's a budget!

Another good thing to do is to start a monthly expenses *tracker* once you have paid your bills. Keep track of the actual amounts you pay out for each monthly bill and the unanticipated expenses you had to cover. Doing so can help you plan for the next year, or at least give yourself a financial cushion so those unanticipated expenses become less of a burden. I'm not sure what is more expensive to maintain – a truck or three cats.

INVESTING –

If possible, set aside money beyond regular checking and savings accounts.

I have a few retirement accounts. Some are through work, where I basically choose between conservative or aggressive investing opportunities by checking a couple of boxes in my benefits profile.

Outside of my works investments, I have a few accounts where I worked with my financial advisor and chose my own stocks to invest in and follow. Here is where I take a not-so-traditional approach to investing. In order to turn a topic I didn't understand very well into something I wanted get involved in, I chose stocks in companies of interest to me. I have shares of Tiffany & Co., Ford Motor Company and the WWE. Yep. I *own* pieces of those companies! Fun *and* liberating, right?

# Setting Up
# Your Own Household

As of this writing, I am in the process of building my own home, so I am still living with my parents. Can I give advice on setting up my own household? I think so. My parents have spent winters away for the past 19 years, so I learned a few things about living on my own while they were gone. Most of these lessons have reinforced my thought when I first changed my W-4; financially it just does not pay to be single.

My former husband and I had very similar yearly salaries. We both had good, full-time jobs, and were DINKs (Double Income, No Kids). I had become accustomed to a pretty comfortable lifestyle; and except for being able to drive around in a Bentley Mulsanne, we pretty much could afford to do and have what we wanted. That changed once we got divorced. Even though I had a steady, good-paying job, I needed to have a sit-down with myself and determine if there were things I did or had I could no longer afford. I had to set priorities for my living expenses.

Sometimes I think wiping my ex-husband off the planet would have been the better solution. Just kidding. But... I would not have to deal with knowing he had moved on while I struggled with just existing. And, if I had wiped him off the planet, I wouldn't have to worry about finances, grocery shopping and finding a new place to live. The State would have provided all those things for me.

I kid. Kinda.

# Things I Had to Learn

CLEANING –

Remember when I told you S. handled the finances so I was happy to be assigned to cleaning the toilets? I had no idea how dirty those toilets actually were until I no longer lived with a dude in the house. I understand we girls get to sit down to pee, but is that thing so hard to control that boys can't hit a bowl they are standing right on top of? Is peeing like being at the end of a high-pressure fire hose? I guess so, because I no longer had to worry about cleaning up dried on gunk on the sides of the toilet or on the floor around the bowl once it was just me using the bathrooms. This remains one of the mysterious differences between girls and boys, and between keeping the finances or cleaning the toilets—I may have had the more difficult job!

A two-person household has a lot of clutter compared to a one-person household. Mainly, I can see what the surface of my dining room table looks like now that S. isn't there to put nearly everything he owned upon it. He even put his shoes up there. What's worse? The cats on the table, or his shoes & gym bag. I'm sure the cats were cleaner.

## NO MORE DISAPPEARING ITEMS –

Once S. left the house, I witnessed a small miracle. If I went out, the 'things' in our house did not move about while I was gone. My glasses were on the counter, right where I left them. The water glass I kept near the fridge to remind me to stay hydrated stayed put, too. I didn't have to worry about tracking down my shoes or searching high and low for my lipstick. Everything was right where I left it last. Unless it was a small, shiny something, like my earrings or bracelets. Those, unfortunately, usually became cat diversions and ended up under the couch.

## GROCERY SHOPPING -

I hate grocery shopping. S. used to do all of it. Sometimes I would tag along, but more often he did this weekly chore on Sunday mornings so I could sleep in a bit. At first I thought it was because he didn't like my dilly-dallying while we shopped; but looking back, I now think it was because he might not have spent Sunday morning where he said he was—the grocery store. But I digress...

My outlook on grocery shopping is worse than hate. I LOATHE grocery shopping. The first few times I tried shopping on my own, I became so overwhelmed with the whole ordeal I started sobbing in the middle of the Produce Department, had to abandon my shopping cart and bolt for the car. I have no idea why, but it happened—twice. So instead of making yet another scene in the Produce Department, I stopped grocery shopping.

If I needed food, I hit a fast food joint on the way home from work. I drank milk a lot, but would just grab a gallon at the gas station convenience store. If some of my co-workers were hitting the store on lunch, I'd tag along and get a few things, like Pop Tarts, which I considered a full meal. This set-up suited me just fine, but my sister started to notice the food in the cupboards was dwindling, and the only things left in the refrigerator were milk, Diet Coke and a few random condiments. So, she took me grocery shopping on the weekends.

The first time we went grocery shopping together, I was too in awe of her shopping expertise to become overwhelmed in the Produce Department. My sister was a grocery-getting-ninja. She shopped with the precision and determination of a battle worn general. She had a list. She got ONLY what was on her list, and each item was listed and sorted—by aisle. When she found one item on her list and put it in the cart, she crossed the item off her list and moved on to the next. Imagine that? It seemed so easy, yet I was astounded by her serious grocery shopping skills.

I did not have a list. I tried shopping by memory, but found myself getting distracted by what I thought I needed and what I would put into the cart. This thoroughly frustrated my shopping sensei, and she let me know I needed to get more organized. Though we made it through my first foray into 'solo' grocery shopping fairly well, I made sure the next weekend I had a list. Granted, it wasn't as precise as my sister wanted it to be and it was sorted by the item's location at my house, not the grocery store aisles, but it was a start. I make better grocery shopping lists now, but I still loathe grocery shopping. To me, if I'm not buying cute shoes, it seems like a waste of time and money.

Part of the reason I dislike grocery shopping is the actual food buying. Because it was just me consuming the food I bought, I was forever throwing rotting food away. What was good food when I bought it, turned into some weird science project in the fridge because I didn't eat it fast enough? I took some of the practical advice of my fellow divorcees when setting up my new household.

Invest in a good FREEZER—and lots of freezer safe bags and containers. You see, even by reducing my household from two people to one, it totally blew my grocery bill. The freezer became my new best friend. Before I was living on my own, I thought it was just for ice cream. Now I use the freezer to keep from throwing away most of the food I buy each week! Loaves of bread no longer get moldy and gross. Now they get divided into quarters and frozen in smaller freezer bags, so I only use a few pieces of bread at a time. Fresh fruits and veggies get the freezer treatment, too. I can use them for weeks instead of eating a few and throwing the rest onto the compost pile. I buy frozen meals or pre-made meals and freeze them for more dinners later on. Even my favorite—pizza—can be divided and repackaged. Eat a few slices now and keep the rest of it frozen to eat later. Who knew?!

After I have brought all my groceries into the kitchen, I take a few minutes to put multi-pack items like meats and produce into smaller freezer bags, label them with the item and date and put them in the freezer. Sure, it takes a little extra time. But – because I have gotten the hang of meal planning and buying in bulk and then freezing, I make less frequent trips to the grocery store! Score!

Now if I could just figure out how to freeze lettuces. Even if I eat like a rabbit for days on end, I am forever throwing wilted salad greens away.

LAUNDRY -

Another task I don't like? Laundry. My aversion to laundry isn't as deeply rooted as the one to grocery shopping, but I still don't enjoy it. Either I am a really clean person or a really dirty one. The line between the two gets blurred on the floor of the laundry room. When S. and I were married, we did a TON of laundry. Usually on Sundays, we did about six loads. I say we, as it was a team effort. I started the laundry, got bored with it, and he would pick it up and do a couple of loads, too. Then late Sunday night, we'd figure out if we wanted clean clothes for the week, we'd better finish up the last loads and fold it all. It was a vicious cycle!

Having a one-person household presented a new laundry dilemma. How many articles of dirty clothing make up a load? Is there enough laundry to wash weekly or not? Do I really need to sort darks and whites, if there isn't enough of each to warrant washing two loads?

The answer to the last question is a resounding yes. Unless you want all the clothes in that particular load to resemble the darkest article in the washer, separate out those lighter items!

In your new single life, you will discover one liberating thing about laundry. It can wait! At least it can wait until you have enough clothes to make decent-sized loads – or until you run out of clean panties.

# Practical Advice

ROTATE.

What do I mean by rotate? I come from a very extensive retail background. When stocking shelves at the store, we were taught to rotate our stock. When bringing new product out to the sales floor and putting it on the shelf, we pulled the existing stock off the shelf, put the new stock to the back and then replaced the older stock at the front. This way the older stock gets sold first. After becoming a household of one, I learned I needed to do this not only with groceries, but also with things like dishes and bath towels. Nothing will remind you of how lonely you are than using and washing the same damn bowl and spoon every single day. So, rotate them. When you wash that stupid bowl, place it at the bottom of the stack and use a new one the next day.

This is especially important with bath towels. After the towels and washcloths are laundered, rotate them on the shelf in the linen closest so all your bath linens get the same amount of wear each time you use them. No one likes to dry themselves with a scratchy towel, right?

MOVING STUFF can be hard for one person. Especially big, heavy stuff. S. was a very good schlepper. If we needed something moved or carried from Point A to

Point B, he took care of it. Once I was on my own, I had to figure out a way to move things, or just let the big stuff sit. Because I have three cats, moving things to find lost jewelry or remove cat hair from the premises was a must. Short of hiring Two Men and a Truck every weekend to move the living room & dining room furniture from one side of the room and back, I was going to have to figure out a way to move stuff on my own. In the quest to make moving heavy objects less of an obstacle, I found one of the greatest inventions EVER. Furniture glides! I'm pretty sure a very resourceful divorced woman invented furniture glides. The glides are little round discs. When placed under large pieces of furniture, they allow ONE person to move furniture across the floor with minimal effort. You will feel just like She-Ra!

A moving dolly is also a necessity to help you move things around. Make sure you have one of these when you are living on your own. I use it for everything from setting up holiday decorations to helping with large boxes of cat litter.

If all else fails and you still haven't been able to move the living room couch, schedule a Girl's Night Out with happy hour starting at your house. Once all the ladies get there, bribe them with wine so they'll help you rearrange your living room before you go out.

# Bonus (Wonderful) Lessons

Enjoy the MIDDLE! The middle of the bed, the middle of the garage, the middle of the couch. There isn't anything wrong with being a little greedy when defining my space now that I am on my own. I've enjoyed taking up the middle of spaces I used to have to share with my ex-husband, even though I still share most of those spaces with the cats.

I have the POWER! C'mon shout it like She-Ra! Once S. left the house, he no longer controlled the things he left behind. He no longer controlled the remote on the TV. He no longer controlled the thermostat. He didn't control any of the other decisions either. Everything was up to me and ONLY me. I did indeed have the POWER!!!

Speaking of power, I discovered something else would make me feel more em-POWER-ed. Power tools! My dad is a retired contractor. He still builds things and has a very extensive tool collection. In the haste to get moved out of my marital home, I didn't do a very good job of checking for tools in the garage. My former husband was kind enough to put together a rusty old tool-box and fill it with an assortment of implements that looked like they came from the Island of Misfit Tools. He set it by the back door and labeled it 'Tami's Toolbox.' None of the power tools were set aside for me.

I guess he figured since I was a girl, I didn't get to take any of those with me. Even though many of those power tools were gifts from my dad.

While I was living with my parents, dad's garage shop was now open to me, and I rediscovered my love for POWER! Power screwdrivers, drills, and when feeling brave, the saws.

The best thing about being on my own – I made *all* the decisions. Yes, I sought advice from my parents and support network, especially on the Big Stuff, but since it was just me, I had the freedom to do as I pleased. I did feel a tinge of guilt the first time I decided to sit around in my PJs all day on a snowy Sunday, as in the past staying in PJs later in the day would have been unacceptable. S. always had to be doing something or going somewhere, which meant I had to go along with his plans. So, the first time I was in my new house late on a Sunday afternoon, still in my pajamas, I thought, *What have I done?* But my sister and friends assured me wasting one day every once in a while, was a good thing to do.

I didn't have to hesitate in making decisions on what I wanted to do. No longer did I have to ask, *Where do you want to go? What do you want to eat? How should we spend the weekend?* Sure, if I was going out with other people, I had to take other opinions into consideration, but if it was just me picking a place to grab a bite to eat, I got to make the decision. Not him. Not anyone else – just me. At first it was a little scary, but now making all the decisions might be difficult to give up. I have become truly independent.

# Chapter Eight
## Closure

**What it is and where to find it.**

I think Closure hangs out with Sasquatch and the Loch Ness Monster drinking from the Holy Grail while they watch unicorns and mermaids play under a sky filled with UFOs somewhere near Atlantis. Slightly elusive, Closure is. So elusive, in fact, many of us who go through divorce doubt its very existence. That's how I felt about Closure. And I discovered there are two ways of dealing with it.

> One—Break out the Indiana Jones kit and start the quest to find this mysterious thing, creature and/or place; or,
>
> Two—Admit Closure might not want to be found right away and take comfort in knowing it is out there waiting to be discovered.

Maybe Closure isn't a mythical creature or something legends are made of, but it's not easy to find; and people often describe different experiences once they do find it. Similar stories are told about witness reports of UFO sightings. Everyone saw *something*, but each person had a different version of events of what happened and what the UFO looked like.

Because S. refused to attend therapy with me while we were going through the divorce, he never answered my question of what was making him so unhappy. He never told me why he wanted to leave me or what I had done wrong. I now know I didn't do anything wrong, but still I haven't gotten any closer to that thing called Closure.

For my family, Closure may never be found. S. never said anything to my parents or my sister. He never apologized, tried to explain, or even said good-bye. My mother is hurt. My father is angry. My sister would have helped me pay for his one-way ticket to the Seventh Circle of Hell.

I'm not sure I'll ever find Closure, but I have been able to find similar creatures that aren't quite as elusive—Comfort and Peace. There is Comfort knowing I didn't want this divorce and did everything I could to fix things before throwing in the towel. As I've often said, my marriage didn't fail; my ex-husband failed our marriage.

There is Comfort with his family. Are we as close as we used to be? No. Will there ever be a time where we will love each other as much as we did when S. and I were still together? Most likely not. But I am comfortable knowing they have a pretty good idea this divorce wasn't what I wanted, and I would have done anything to remain a part of the family.

There is Comfort in knowing I am surrounded by people who want me to succeed in my new, post-divorce life. They want me to be happy and help me be brave as I navigate these unknown waters called the Sea of Independence.

Then there is Peace. Peace isn't quite as stable as Comfort, but it is more poignant. Peace is doing things I enjoy again. Sitting on the porch swing in the evenings, thinking about my future and no longer being afraid. Going to restaurants and places where S. and I used to go, and not feeling like a dark cloud was following me there. Knitting, reading, watching TV—doing all these things without feeling anxious and alone. In each of these things I have found Peace because I was able to leave the painful reminders of S. behind. I won't sugar coat it. Without Closure, Peace sometimes gets knocked around a bit. For the most part, I have found Peace with my current situation.

Peace has a companion, Solitude. I used to be afraid of Solitude. When I was married, I never had to worry about Solitude, as my ex-husband equated it with idleness, which just wasn't allowed. When I lived in my parents' home after the divorce I was around other people 24/7, so there weren't a lot of quiet moments then, either. As I adjust to life on my own, there have been a few times where I sat down, looked around and quoted the song from the Talking Heads, that one where David Byrne is asking, "How did I get here?" I ask Solitude the question, but get only silence. And that is OK, as sometimes (wait for it!) silence is golden. I am learning to embrace Solitude. You will, too.

# Time Travel

One of the guiding principles of time travel is the traveler must never come in contact with its past self, as it puts a wrinkle in the time/space continuum. Or something. When I was going through my divorce, though, I really wish my future self would have been there to warn me. I didn't want to go all the way back to July 14, 1990 (my wedding day) as I still considered it to be the happiest day of my life. I just wished my former self could have warned me about the divorce and told me to hang on tight, as I was about to encounter a pretty bumpy ride.

Time may not completely heal *all* wounds, but perhaps it does soften the edges. In that vein, I wrote a letter to the me who was blindsided on the day my marriage started to unravel.

February 1st – a couple of years after the divorce decree:

Dear Tami,

I understand you received some devastating news today. Your husband of nearly twenty-three years told you he doesn't think he loves you anymore and he no longer wants to be married to you.

It's going to take some time for you to come to terms with what he told you today. I'm here to tell you no matter what you are feeling right now, things are going to be OK. It will take time, what on many days may seem like an eternity, but you will get through this and be OK.

You need to remember one thing. This is not your fault. You didn't cause this and you didn't want anything to do with getting a divorce.

As time goes on, you will realize even though you don't think S. handled things right, he didn't deal with his own demons before throwing them at you, he was right about one thing— he is going to tell you even though this divorce is being forced on you, how you react to it and how you deal with it is entirely up to you. And you will deal with this in the right way, with grace and dignity.

Speaking of him, you are about to discover some very unnerving things about your former husband. You will uncover details about him that will cut you to the core and make you question the last twenty-three or more years of your life. Be careful. Dwelling on what he has done will not help you move forward. Questioning his motives, his reasons, won't help either. As your future therapist, Dr. Help, will tell you, "Accepting it doesn't mean liking it." You don't have to like what is happening to you, but eventually you must accept it.

I won't kid you— getting to acceptance won't be easy. You'll feel a range of emotions like anger (and even hate) that are not familiar to you. It won't happen overnight. It will take nearly three years from today for you to feel fairly normal. Even then, there will be days where you sit down and ask yourself, "How did I get here? This is not where I am supposed to be." But it is where you are and everything is going to be OK.

As you go through the next several months, know this, your heart is true and this fact alone will draw others to you. Rely on those around you and realize it is OK to ask for their help.

Though you will now be called things like ex-wife, divorcee and (brace yourself) single, this divorce will not define you. You will be able to use your experience and everything you learned along the way to help other women going through divorces, too. Like you keep telling yourself and others, "Something good must come out of all of this." And something good will.

In time, you will walk tall again. Your smile will return and you will laugh. You may not see it now, but you will shine. Rely on your inner light to get you through those darkest days.

Don't get distracted or distraught over what you hear about him, Tami. What he does has no bearing on you now. Let karma stay the course. What happens to him is no longer your concern. Let him suffer his own consequences.

Right now, you need to concentrate on the road ahead. I'll be waiting for you at the end of the road with a special toast to the new, strong woman you have become.

Tami Jayne

Even though you can't begin to imagine this, you will be (I am) better off without him.

Wishing you love, laughter and happiness,
Tami

# Never Question Mother

My first real-life lesson still holds true – Mom is always right. Even though I spent most of my life trying to deny it. After my divorce, my mom's sage advice to me whenever I got stuck in one of my *why is this happening to me?* moods was:

The only way to move is forward.

At first, I would grit my teeth at those words, and again question my mother's wisdom, but eventually I came to realize she was right. So, my advice to you:

Girl, get moving! Just put one foot in front of the other...

# Recommended Reading and Resources

**Divorce in General**

No books or websites will help you nearly as much as your support network and fellow divorcees, but here are some books to keep in mind, too.

*Not Your Mother's Divorce* – Kay Moffett & Sarah Touborg

*Crazy Time* – Abigail Trafford

*The Divorced Girl's Society* – Vicki King & Jennifer O'Connell

**Legal Advice**

Be sure to do an internet search of Legal Resources & Attorneys in your area. It's helpful to have legal information pertinent to your situation and region.

You'll note there are no books here. I tried reading a couple books that addressed divorce proceedings. They were not easy reads. It was better for me to seek legal advice from real people.

**Wellbeing**

*The Book of Stress Survival* – Alix Kirsta

*The Handbook of Tai Chi* – Ray Pawlett

WebMD.com – If you are borderline hypochondriac, you have no business going to this website. Stay off the computer! By the way, divorce will not give you the Measles or Lyme disease. My doctor checked.

Livestrong.com – Free drug advice, maybe? Sorry, my bad. It really is a very helpful website for overall wellbeing.

Fitnessblender.com

Gaiam.com

Choosemyplate.gov

Thecenterformindfuleating.org

## Financial Advice

Daveramsey.com

Mr. Ramsey also has a bunch of books – all very helpful if you are not familiar with maintaining your finances. If I had to pick favorites, if there is such a thing when dealing with finances, I would choose:

*The Complete Money Makeover*

*The Money Answer Book*

Don't forget to do some fun reading, too! Like Shakespeare or something.